Bhajanamritam

Devotional songs of Sri Mata Amritanandamayi

Volume 4

Mata Amritanandamayi Center
San Ramon, California, United States

Bhajanamritam

Volume 4

Published by:

Mata Amritanandamayi Center
P.O. Box 613
San Ramon, CA 94583-0613
USA

In India:
www.amritapuri.org
inform@amritapuri.org

In USA:
www.amma.org

In Europe:
www.amma-europe.org

Contents

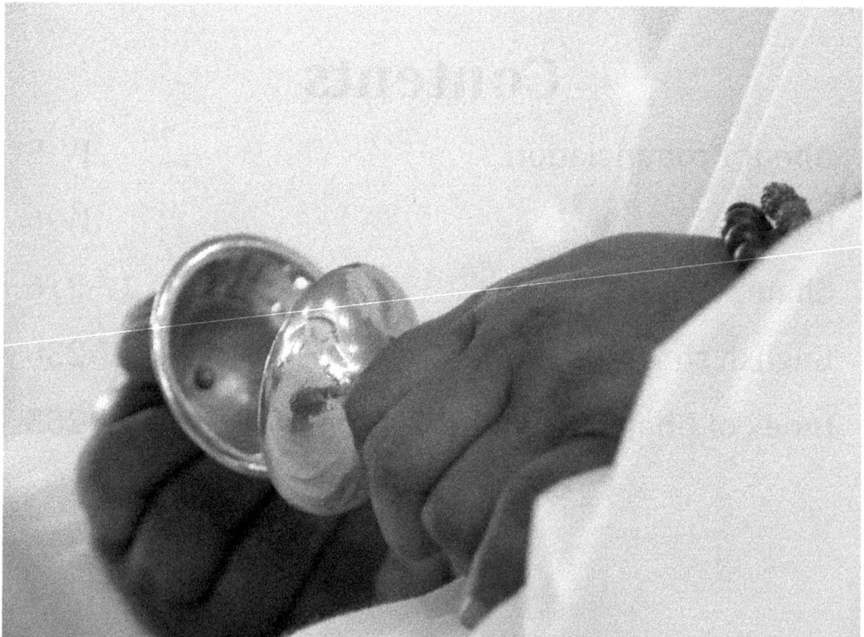

About Pronunciation

The following key is for the guidance of those who are unfamiliar with the Sanskrit and Malayalam transliteration codes which are used in this book:

A	-as	a	in <u>A</u>merica
AI	-as	ai	in <u>ai</u>sle
AU	-as	ow	in h<u>ow</u>
E	-as	e	in th<u>ey</u>
I	-as	ea	in h<u>ea</u>t
O	-as	o	in <u>o</u>r
U	-as	u	in s<u>u</u>it
KH	-as	kh	in Ec<u>kh</u>art
G	-as	g	in <u>g</u>ive
GH	-as	gh	in lo<u>gh</u>ouse
PH	-as	ph	in she<u>ph</u>erd
BH	-as	bh	in clu<u>bh</u>ouse
TH	-as	th	in lig<u>th</u>ouse
DH	-as	dh	in re<u>dh</u>ead
C	-as	c	in <u>c</u>ello
CH	-as	ch-h	in staun<u>ch-h</u>eart
JH	-as	dge	in he<u>dge</u>hog
Ñ	-as	ny	in ca<u>ny</u>on
Ś	-as	sh	in <u>sh</u>ine
Ṣ	-as	c	in effi<u>c</u>ient
Ṅ	-as	ng	in si<u>ng</u>, (nasal sound)
V	-as	v	in <u>v</u>alley, but closer to a "w"
ZH	-as	rh	in <u>rh</u>ythm

Vowels which have a line on top of them are long vowels, they are pronounced like the vowels listed above but are held for twice the amount of time.

The letters with dots under them (ṭ, ṭh, ḍ, ḍh, ṇ, l, ṣ) are palatal consonants, they are pronounced with the tip of the tongue against the hard palate. Letters without such dots are dental consonants and are pronounced with the tongue against the base of the teeth.

Bhajans

ĀDIŚAKTI BRAHMĀMṚTA

Ādiśakti brahmāmṛta rūpiṇī
ammayāyi vanniraṅgi bhūtalē
kanmaṣaṅgal mātti nēr vazhīykku nī
ñaṅgale nayikkuvān pirannu nī

O primeval power, bliss of Brahman incarnate, You have descended to the Earth in the form of the Mother. To cleanse us of our sins and guide us along the true path You have come.

Jātimata cintakal marannu nām
makkalāyi onnu cērnnu ninnu nām
kāladēśa bhittikal takarnnahō
śānti tan pularī vannudichitā

Having become one, united as Your children, we have forgotten all divisive thoughts of caste and religion. The walls of time and space are crumbling down and the dawn of peace has arrived.

Svapna lōka tullyamām jagattitil
snēhavarṣiṇi nīyum vannuvō
makkale tuṇaykkuvān uṇarttuvān
tyāgamūrttiyāyi nī jaganmayī

O loving Mother, You have come to this dream-like world to rescue and redeem us, Thy children. You are the Mother of the universe and the embodiment of self-sacrifice.

Sarva dukha hāriṇi mahēśvarī
sarva saukyadāyini amṛtēśvarī

sarvapāpanāśanam nin darśanam
sarvadā labhikkuvān tozhunnu ñān

You remove all sorrows and bestow all wishes, all-powerful, immortal Goddess. The vision of You purifies us of all sins; I prostrate to have that vision always.

ĀDIṢĒṢA ANANTA ṢAYANA

Ādiṣēṣa ananta ṣayana
śrīnivāsa śrī vēnkatēṣa

O Vishnu, lying in ananta shayana, on the bed formed by the great serpent king Adishesha. You dwell in Lakshmi's heart, O Lord Venkatesha.

Pannaga bhūṣaṇa kailasa vasa
gauri patē śambhō śamkara
gauri patē śambhō hara hara

Adorned with snakes, residing in Kailas, Lord of Gauri, Shambo Shamkara, Shiva.

Yadukula bhūṣaṇa yaśōdā tanaya
rādha patē gōpālā kṛṣṇā

Gem of the Yadava dynasty, son of Yashoda, the Lord of Radha, O cowherd boy, Krishna.

Raghukula tilaka raghu rāmacandra
sītā patē śrī rāmacandra

The foremost of the Raghu Dynasty, Ramachandra, the Lord of Sita, Lord Rama.

Pandarināthā pānduranga
jay jay viṭṭhala jaya hari viṭṭhala

Lord of Pandari, Panduranga, victory to Vittala.

AKATĀRILARIVINTE

Akatārilarivinte
olinālam telichu
avirāmam vijayippor-
abhirāma mūrttē

You light the lamp of knowledge in the heart, O ever-victorious one, O personification of beauty.

Amṛtēśvarī ennil
uṇarum vīcāraṅgal
amṛta sughandhikal ākkū

Immortal Goddess, let the thoughts that arise in me possess the fragrance of nectar.

Kuññilam tennalāl
tenni vīṇuṭayunna
maññilam tulliyānente janmam
eṅkilumāyattil ūyalāṭunniten
āśakal tāraka pūvirukkān

My life is fragile like a tender dewdrop. If stirred even by a small breeze it shall fall. Yet my reckless desires swing high to pluck the stars as if they were flowers.

Vākkil kurukum porulinte pūrṇṇataykkā
ātmavilūṭartha rāśi tētum
tīrthāṭakan ñān namikkunnu cinmayī
vākkum vicāravum snigdhamākkū

By searching for the inner Self, I try to find the complete truth conveyed in profound words. I am a mere pilgrim, O embodiment of knowledge; I prostrate before You. Make my words and thoughts sweet.

AKATTIL IRRUPPAVALE

Akattil iruppavale ammā
nilattai valarppavale
manattil tiruvaṭi makizhnta ninaittida
valatte tarupavale

O Mother, You are the indweller of my heart. You, who bestow every good, please grant the boon to blissfully remember Your lotus feet, O Goddess of Amritapuri.

Kaṭalin alaitazhavum tennai
kavitai mazhai pozhiyum
maṭalin maṇam kamazhum anke
annai mukham teriyum
amṛtapurēśvariye ammā
mangala nāyakiyē

Where the waves gently sweep the shore of the sea, where the palm trees sing poetry in the wind, where the flowers share their beautiful fragrance, there the resplendent face of Mother is manifested.

Amṛta puriyinile antru
pirantatum nī tāne
kārttikai mātarasi kanintu
koṇṭatum unaittāne

You who were born in Amritapuri, You descended in the Karttika month amongst the devotees.

Uṇmai teriyātā ammā
ullam irankātā
annai pūraṇiyē ammā
mangala nāyakiyē

Are You not the embodiment of Truth? O Mother of the universe, won't You come down to us, You who give auspiciousness to all.

Āyiram itazhkalin mēl ammā
amarntu pārttiṭuvāy
seykalin tuyarkalaiyē dēvi
ceruttu kāttiṭuvāy

Sitting on the thousand-petalled lotus, You look after us all. You diminish the mistakes we commit in our ignorance and thus rescue us.

Ēzhai eliyavaril tāye
ēkkam pōkkiṭuvāy
kōzhai manatinīle koñcam
vīram tanttiṭuvāy

You assuage the grief of the poor and the downtrodden; into the minds of cowards You pour valour.

ĀKHILĀṆḌĒŚVARĪ AMBĒ

Ākhilāṇḍēśvarī ambē
jay mā (4x)
abhayapradāyini ambē
jay mā (4x)

O Mother, the Lord of the entire cosmos, You who grant us refuge, victory to You.

Śakti svarūpini jay mā
hē śubhadāyini jay mā
saṃkaṭa mōcini ambē
jay mā (10x)

The embodiment of power, granting purity and liberating us from sorrow, victory to Mother.

Mangaladāyini jay mā (4x)
mantra vihārini jay mā (4x)
hē śritapālini jay mā
śiva hṛdi vāsini jay mā
atulita rūpini ambē
jay mā (10x)

You who bestow auspiciousness, who embody the sacred mantras and protect those who seek refuge, who dwell in the heart of Shiva, the Mother of incomparable form, victory to the Mother.

AMBĀ BHAVĀNĪ PARĀTPARĒ

Ambā bhavānī parātparē
ambā śivānī dayānidhē
bhavasāgar sē mujche bachāō
abhayahast mujche dījiyē

Mother Bhavani, beyond all, Mother Sivani, the abode of compassion, save me from the ocean of transmigration; give me refuge in You.

Jay jay śamkarī jay abhayamkarī
jay śamkarī jay paramēśvarī
jay jay śamkarī jay bhuvanēśvarī
jay śamkarī jay hṛdayēśvarī

Victory to Sankari, who performs auspicious deeds; victory to You who grant refuge. Victory to the supreme Goddess, the Goddess of the universe, the Goddess of the heart.

Tum hī dēvi jagadādhār
sab jīvōm mē antaryāmī
aviratаśānti barsāō
sakalapāp sē mukt karō

You, O Goddess, are the substratum of this creation, the indweller of all beings. Shower unending peace upon me, O Goddess; free me from all sins.

Guṇ gātā hum tērē mātē
hṛday tumhārā dhām banāō
śaraṇāgat kō śaraṇ mē lē lō
paramaprēm bharō man mē māyē

I sing Your glories, O Mother, make my heart Your abode. Grant me eternal refuge in You. O Maya, fill my mind with supreme love.

AMMĀ AMMĀ BHAIRAVIYĒ

Ammā ammā bhairaviyē
amṛtānandamayī śāmbhaviyē
ammā tripura sundariyē
ānanda vaṭivē īśvariyē

Mother, wife of Siva, embodiment of immortal bliss, there is none more beautiful than You in all the three worlds. Great Goddess, You are the embodiment of happiness.

Amṛtānanda mayamānāy
akhilam kākkum tāyānāy
kamale vimale bhagavatiyē
kāli gauri vallaviyē

Overflowing with immortal bliss, You are the Mother protecting the entire world. O lotus-like one, pure one, You are Bhagavati, Kali and Gauri, You are capable of accomplishing everything.

Munivar pōtrum mōhiniyē
mukkaṇ nāyaki mīnāṭci
kanivāy arulum karpakamē
kaṭaikkaṇ pārppāy jñānāṭci

The great Sages praise Your enchanting form, O consort of the three-eyed one (Siva). Gracefully appear and bless us. Simply by glancing with the corner of Your eye of wisdom You bestow all desired boons.

Kadamba vanattil uyarmakalē
kanaka valli tirumakalē
kadamba mālai punaipavalē
karppūra dīpam ērppavalē

O great one, resident of Kadamba forest, golden one, master of all wealth, You wear the garland made of Kadamba flowers and accept the camphor light waved before You.

Gangai karaiyil viśālākṣi
kāñci nagaril kāmāṭci
pomkum kāviri ātrōram
pūkkum paśum pon unatāṭci

You are the Goddess Vishalakshi on the shores of the Ganga; You are Kamakshi in the city of Kanci. All the flourishing riches on the shore of the rising Kaveri River are due to Your grace alone.

AMMĀ KĪ CHĀYĀ MĒ

Ammā kī chāyā mē mērā saphar
yē tērī kṛpā hē mērī mā
kitanē pāp mēnē kiyē
tū nē mujhē phir bhī apanāyā

The journey of life is in Mother's protective and cool shade. This is only by the grace of my Mother. How many sins have I committed? Even then, You have taken me as Your own, my Mother.

Jaltī huyī naklī galiyō mē
bhaṭaka rahā thā mērī mā
pyār ki ik bunda kē liyē
taḍapa rahā thā jagadambā

In the hot, burning streets of delusion, O Mother, I was wandering aimlessly. O Mother of the universe, I was longing in agony for one drop of love.

Duniyā kē māyā sāgar mē
ḍūb rahā thā mērī mā
bālō sē pakaḍa kē mujhē
kaisē bacāyā jagadambā

I was drowning in the illusionary ocean that constitutes this world. O my Mother, catching me by the hair, how did You manage to save me?

Tujhē mē kyā dē sakū
tērē bāg kā paudhā mā
śabnam banē mērē āsū
tērē caraṇō pē arpit mā

What can one such as I possibly offer to You, Mother? I am just a small sapling in Your garden; my tears have become dew drops. I surrender these at Your feet.

AMMĀ UN PUNNAGAYIL

Ammā un punnagayil
ulakamellām mayankidumē
ammā un tiruvadiyil
akhilamellām odunkidumē

Mother, by Your divine smile the whole world becomes enchanted; into Your holy feet the whole creation merges.

Pārve ontrē pōtum ammā
tī vinaikal ōdidumē
kanivudanē kaṇpārttu
piravikkadal kadattiduvāy

A glance of grace from You is enough to dispel all evil destiny. With Your divine gaze, take me across the ocean of birth and death.

Vēlēntum kaumāri atai
vem puṇṇil pāychāmal
vēṇdiyate tantaruli
vilankiduvāy en manatil

O Goddess Kaumari, You who wield the spear, do not poke Your spear into my infected and bleeding wounds. Please bestow upon me that which is good for me and shine forever in my heart.

Vēṇdām ini piravi ontrum
pirantālō vēṇdu vatu
nīnkāmal un ninaivil
nilaittirukum gati vēṇdum

I do not desire to be born again. But if I happen to be born again, let it be a birth in which I will always be established in the remembrance of You.

ammā amṛtēśvarīye

AMMA YUPĒKṢA

Ammayupēkṣa kāṇichīṭukil pinne
kuññinu gatiyuṇṭō
amma mukham tirichālilam kuññinte
kaṇṇukal tōrnnīṭumō

If Mother neglects Her child, does that child have any other refuge? If Mother turns Her face away, will the child's eyes ever be dry?

Amma tan tēn mozhi kātōrttu
nilkumī kuññine yōrkukillē
kālum manassil kulirmazha peyumā
nādamutil kukillē

Won't You remember this child who is eagerly waiting, with rapt attention, to hear Your nectarous words? Won't You speak those words - like rainfall to a burning mind?

Vēdanakal tande bhāṇavumāyilam
paitalaṇaṇiṭunnu
vēdavēdāntaṅgal vāzhtti stutikkuna
mātāvu nīyaliyillē

This small child comes to You with a bundle of sorrows. O Mother, who is praised and extolled by the Vedas and Upanishads, won't You be merciful?

Vērpāṭin dukhamām vēnalil nīyoru
varṣamāy vannaṇayū
viṅgum manassumāy vāṭikkariṇṇiṭum
vallikalkamṛtu peyu

Come to me like a downpour in the scorching summer of the sadness of separation. Please pour some nectar on the creepers that are burnt and wilted.

AMṚTA DĀYINIYAMMĒ

Amṛta dāyiniyammē anupamaguṇa nidhē
avikala śānti nalkū abhayapradē
azhivillā jñāna jyōtinilayamē nirupamē
akhilarum vāzhttunnu nin apadānaṅgal

O Mother, overflowing with bliss, You are the treasure house of unequalled merit. Please grant me eternal peace, O You who provide refuge. Storehouse of immeasurable, luminous knowledge, incomparable one, all beings join together in praise of Your glorious deeds.

Azhakezhum mukhapatmam akatāril viriyumbōl
azhalellām kozhiyum vannilla kaivarum
pārijāta kusumattinnābhavellum padāmbujē
pārilellām parakkaṭṭe ninte vaibhavam

When Your radiant smile illumines my mind, all sorrows will vanish and I will soar to divine heights. Your tender feet surpass even the parijata flower of paradise in beauty. May Your greatness be known throughout the world.

Maruvuka satatam nī mānasamām śrī kōvilil
marataka maṇivarṇṇē mamatāpaḥē
caritārtthan āvaṭṭe nin caraṇa smaraṇayālē
kaniyuka dēvi nityam anugrahikū

You shine with the luster of an emerald; destroyer of attachments, reside in the temple of my heart. May I be blessed with the remembrance of Your sacred feet. Bestow Your compassion, O Goddess, grant me Your eternal blessings.

AMṚTAKALĒ ĀNANDAKALĒ

Amṛtakalē ānandakalē
avikalajīvita dānaratē
hēmalatē suralōkanutē
nikhila manohara dānaratē

O Mother, You are the embodiment of eternal bliss. Bestower of unblemished life, You are the golden Goddess worshipped by the eternal world of celestials. You grant all of the desires of our hearts.

Ammē śaraṇam dēvi śaraṇam
jay jay kāli kapālini śaraṇam (2x)

We take refuge in Mother, we take refuge in Devi. We take refuge in Kali, victory to Kali.

Sāmanutē samgītaratē
vēdapurāṇa payōdhisudhē
śōkaharē kalipāpaharē
śuka nārada pūjita pādayutē

O Mother, the divine songs of the scriptures worship You who always revel in music. You are the nectar of the vast ocean of the Vedas and the Puranas. You remove all of our grief and our sins. Your sacred feet are worshipped even by the great Sages.

Śrī lalitē girirājasutē
śruti mantra vihāriṇi mañjupadē

śivaramaṇi śubha bhāvayutē
śrī nāthā sahōdari haimavati

O Lalitha, daughter of the king of the mountains, You dwell in the sacred mountain of the Vedas. Darling of Shiva, You are full of auspiciousness. You are the sister of Lord Vishnu and the daughter of Himavan.

Prēmamayī praṇatābhayadē
karuṇāmṛta varṣiṇi guhajananī
jaya jananī jagatām jananī
jaya kālikapālini mantramayī

O Mother, embodiment of love, You grant refuge to Your supplicants. You are the source of infinite compassion and the Mother of Guha. Victory to the Mother of the universe. Victory to Kali, who wears a garland of skulls, the embodiment of sacred mantras.

AMṚTAMAYĪ PRĒMAMAYĪ

Amṛtamayī prēmamayī
amṛtānandamayī amṛtānandamayī

Immortal one, embodiment of love, You are established in immortal bliss.

Sarvvamayī sarvēśvaryamayī
satcinmayī cinmayī

You are the Lord and the essence of all, the embodiment of truth and knowledge.

Arivē arivinnuravē tava
smitamē iha āgamam
manamē mana mōhinī smaraṇam
śōka mōha vināśanam

You glow with the effulgence of knowledge; the Vedas are Your smile. You who manifest as the mind, enchantress, the remembrance of You destroys all sorrow and delusion.

Amṛtē amṛtakalayē [kalayē ātmanilayē]
ennarikil varika śubhadē [lasitē prēmalasitē]
taru nī oru varam nī
śiva vāma bhāganilayē

O immortal Goddess, eternel one, do come near me. Bestower of auspiciousness, grant me a boon, You who adorn the left side of Siva.

AMṚTĀNANDAM CORIYUNNAMMĒ

Amṛtānandam coriyunnammē
hṛdaya sarassil śrutiyāy
gītamāy bhavamāy nī nirayū

You are the Mother who bestows immortal bliss; fill the clear essence of my heart with Your melodious song of love.

Malarin maṇamāṇu nī en
manassil dhanamāṇu nī
kavibhāvanayāy viṭarunnammē
madhurita cintayuṇarttu ninnuṭe
surabhila cintayuṇarttū

O wealth of the mind, fragrance of the flower, You bloom in my mind as poetic inspiration. Awaken my soul with Your sweet, fragrant thoughts.

Kanivin kaṭalāṇu nī ammē
azhal pōkkum arivāṇu nī
avirāmam aviṭutte gatiyācikkunnu
oru pūjāsūnamāy svīkarikkū enne

tavapūjā sūnamāy svīkarikkū

Ocean of compassion, You are the knowledge which destroys sorrows. This orphan entreats You to take him up as a flower for You to offer in Your worship.

AMṚTA VĀHINI

Amṛta vāhiniyāyiṭṭavaniyil avatari-
chamarum nāyikē ninne kai vaṇaṅgunnēn
śruti yuktyanūbhavaṅgal orumichu vilayicho-
ratulya sundara rūpam vijayichālum

Salutations to that great leader who has incarnated on this Earth as the vehicle of immortality. Victory unto that incomparable and beautiful form that is the embodiment of reason, of experience and of all the knowledge that is contained in the Vedas.

Titti tāra titti tai ti tai taka tai tai tom
Tai tai tai tai tai tai tai tai titai taka tai tai tom
Titti tāra titti tai ti tai taka tai tai tom
Titti tāra titti tai ti tai taka tai tai tom
Mati banda makaluvān pakal iravukal ellām
pāṭu peṭunnavar kkennum abhaya dātri
atiratta karuṇayō ṭamaruṇitā namukkum
paramātma swabōdhatte yuṇarttīṭuvān

You provide solace to those who struggle day and night to be free from the attachments of the mind. You wait with boundless compassion to awaken the ultimate consciousness in us.

Bhava nadi ttirakale kaṭannozhukuvānini
samayamāy samartthareē pōruka niṅgal
kai piṭichu karēttuvān karuti nilpa tuṇṭamma
kaṇṭuvō nammalkku nanma varuvānāyi

The time has come now to cross over the waves of worldliness. If you are smart enough, come. Don't you see that Mother is ready to hold our hands and pull us to the shore, to bless us with prosperity?

Vrata mantra japamellām vṛthāvil ākilum guru
karuṇatan mizhi tannāl phalam nirṇṇayam
parihasichālum janam pari bhavi kkarutu nām
parama pāvaniye ttān ārādhichālum

Even if all vows and chanting of mantras goes in vain, still if the Guru's compassionate glance is made to fall on us, it will bestow the desired ends. Even though others may make fun of us, don't feel humiliated. Continue to worship this great, pure soul (Mother) alone.

Tikavutto raviṭutte ttiruvullam aliññennāl
tikavinnāy namukku pinnalaññiṭēṇṭā
mananamceytakam teliññuṭal abhimānam nīṅgi
swarūpa sudhārṇavattil turññu pōkām

O Mother! You are of the nature of completeness. If Your heart melts then we need not roam around the world in search of fulfillment. By meditating upon this truth, let us purify our hearts. Shed the feeling "I am the body" and we will go to the Self, rowing through the ocean of nectar.

Atu nukarnnu ṇarumbōl erul alayakalum
pinnakhilāṇdam prabhā pūrṇṇam cinmaya
mākūm

anarghamā matu nēṭān kṣaṇa nēram kalayāte
amṛta vāhiniyil pukkabhayam tēṭū

When we drink that imperishable nectar and awake, then the waves of darkness will disappear and the entire universe will melt into divine light and knowledge. Work for that which is the only thing worth striving for without wasting even one single moment. Seek eternal refuge in the vehicle of immortality!

AMṚTĒŚVARĪ HṚDAYĒŚVARĪ

Amṛtēśvarī hṛdayēśvarī (2x)

Immortal Goddess, Goddess of the heart.

Karuṇā sāgarī amṛtēśvarī
kanivāy varuvāy amṛtēśvarī
kāmākṣi mīnākṣi amṛtēśvarī
kāśi viśālākṣi amṛtēśvarī

O ocean of compassion, show mercy and come before me. You are Kamakshi (Goddess of Kanchi), You are Meenakshi (Goddess of Madurai), You are Kashi Vishalakshi (Goddess of Benares), O immortal Goddess.

Manamē un kōvil amṛtēśvarī
mamgala dēvi amṛtēśvarī
gunamē kāṇikai amṛtēśvarī
kuṅkuma nāyaki amṛtēśvarī

Goddess of auspiciousness, my heart is Your temple, my qualities are the offering, O Goddess of kumkum (vermillon), immortal Goddess.

Dukha nivāriṇi amṛtēśvarī
tudīppōrkkarūl tarum amṛtēśvarī
kaṣta nivāriṇi amṛtēśvarī
kātchi taruvāy amṛtēśvarī

You are the destroyer of all sorrows; anyone who worships You will be blessed. You who remove all of the obstacles in one's path throughout life, please reveal Your form, O immortal Goddess.

AMṚTĒŚVARĪ JAGADĪŚVARĪ HĒ MĀTṚRŪPA

Amṛtēśvarī jagadīśvarī
hē mātṛrūpa mahēśvarī
mamatāmayī karunāmayī
hē mātṛrūpa mahēśvarī

O immortal Goddess, O great empress of the universe, who has come as a Mother, You are full of maternal love and compassion. You are the empress of the universe.

Jagajīvanī sañjīvanī samasta jīvanēśvarī
hē mātṛrūpa mahēśvarī

You are the giver of life to the entire universe, resurrector of all beings, the queen of all souls. You are the empress of the universe who has come as a Mother.

Kṛpālinī jagatāriṇī pratipal bhuvana hṛdayēśvarī
hē mātṛrūpa mahēśvarī

O compassionate one, You who carry all the souls of the universe across the ocean of transmigration, You reign over the hearts of all that dwell on this Earth.

Tamahāriṇi śubhakāriṇi manamōhinī viśvēśvarī

hē mātṛrūpa mahēśvarī

O queen of the world, You are the destroyer of darkness, the cause of all auspiciousness. O enchanter of the mind, You are the empress of the universe who has come as a Mother.

AMṚTĒŚVARĪ ŚRITAPĀLINĪ

Amṛtēśvarī śritapālinī
jagadīśvarī jayabhairavī
mṛtināśinī mamjulē
jayadāyinī śāradē

Goddess of immortality, You grant protection to Your devotees. O Lord of the world, victory to You, Bhairavi. You destroy death, O beautiful one, bestower of victory and the Goddess of learning.

Jananāyakī jayaśamkari
janaraṇjinī śāmbhavī
bhavatārinī bhayahāriṇī
bhuvanēśvarī bhāratī

You are the leader of all of mankind. Victory to You, O Sankari. Giver of delight to all, consort of Siva, You free us from the darkness of transmigration and dispel all fear. Goddess of the Earth, You revel in the light of knowledge.

Śivakāminī śubhakāriṇī
śruti pālinī śrīkarī
svararāgiṇī suranāyakī
sukhadāyanī sundarī

You who long for Siva, You with an auspicious nature, You uphold the Vedas and perform holy deeds. You are the tune and melody of music; You guide even the celestial beings, O bestower of happiness, O beautiful one.

Karunāmayī kalināśinī
kavitāmayī kālikē
guru rūpiṇī girinandinī
gajagāminī ambikē

Embodiment of compassion, You who destroy all wickedness, Goddess of prosperity, Kali, You who have assumed the form of the Guru. Daughter of the mountain, You who stride with the majesty of an elephant, O Mother.

ĀNANDA JANANĪ

Ānanda jananī ātamkaśamanī
ālōla nayanē mā
prēmārdra hṛdayē pūrṇṇēndu vadanē
pīyūṣa nilayē mā

O blissful Mother, the destroyer of sorrows, You are endowed with beautiful eyes, Your heart is softened with love. Your radiant face resembles the full moon, O storehouse of nectar.

Manamōhanāmgī matidānaśīlē
mṛtijanmarahitē mā
maṇipūra nilayē mṛduramya vacanē
madhuvarṣaniratē mā
madhuvarṣaniratē mā

Mother of enchanting form, You are the dispenser of discrimination. Devoid of birth and death, dwelling in the manipurna chakra, O soft-spoken one, You shower honey-like words upon us.

Karuṇaika nilayē suravandya caraṇē
kavi gīta caritē mā
kaivalya sadanē kāvyādi rasikē

kāmēśa dayitē mā
kāmēśa dayitē mā

Fountainhead of compassion, You are praised by the celestial beings and Your glories are sung by poets. Embodiment of liberation, the inspiration behind great literature, You are the consort of Shiva.

Himaśailajātē hṛdayēśidurgē
hēramba jananī mā
viśvaika vandyē vēdantavēdyē
vāgdēvi varadē mā
vāgdēvi varadē mā

O daughter of the Himalayan Mountains, You dwell in our hearts, O Durga. You are the Mother of Ganesha and revered by the whole world. Exemplifying the Upanishadic truths, O Goddess of speech, You dispense boons upon us.

ĀNANDA VĪTHIYILŪDENTE

Ānanda vīthiyilūdente atmāvu
ādi rasichu nadannoru nāl
ā nimiṣaṅgalil rāgādi vairikal
ōdiyolichiten gahvarattil

One day long ago, my soul was dancing in delight through the path of bliss. At that time, all of the inner foes such as attraction and aversion ran away and hid themselves in the innermost recesses of my mind.

Enne maraññu ñān ennilūṭannoru
tankakkināvil layichu
ankurikkunna manasile aśakal
pankamilāte teliññu

Forgetting myself, I merged in a golden dream that arose from within me. Noble aspirations clearly manifested themselves in my mind.

Ponkaravallariyālen nerukayil
amma talōṭukayāyi
ente yī jīvitam ammaykkennōti
namra śiraskayāy ninnu

The Divine Mother of the universe caressed my head with bright, gentle hands. I stood respectfully with my head bowed and I told Divine Mother that my life is dedicated to Her.

Annamma conna mozhikalōrttinnu ñān
nannāyi kōrittarippū
satcinmayī sarvasatya svarūpiṇī
nin vacanaṅgal śravikkām

Today, I tremble with bliss recollecting what Mother said. O pure consciousness, the embodiment of Truth, I will heed Your words!

Mandasmitam tūkiyā divya jyōtiss
ennilēykkāzhnnu layichu
kōṭiyabdaṅgal pinniṭṭa kathakalen
cāru sirayiludichu yarnnu

Smiling, She became a divine effulgence and merged in me. The events of millions of years gone by rose up within me.

Mānava janmam kṛtārtthamākkīṭuka
mālōkarēyennu collān
enmanatāril niraṅgal pakarnnamma
ennōdu tannura ceytu

Mother told me to ask the people to fulfill the purpose of their human birth. My mind blossomed, bathed in the many hued light of divinity.

Annutoṭṭanyamāy kkāṇān kazhiññilla
ellāmentātmāvennōrttu
sarvēśiyōdu layichu naṭannu ñān
sarva bhōga tyaktayāyi

From that day onwards, I was unable to perceive anything as different or separate from my own inner Self, everything was a single unity. Merging with the Divine Mother, I renounced all sense of enjoyment.

Ninnil layikkuka nī manujā
ennamma parañña tatvaṅgal
pāriṭamokke muzhakki naṭannu ñān
pāpikalkkāśrayamēkān

"O man, merge in your Self!" This sublime truth, which Mother said, I proclaim to the whole world. May this give refuge and solace to those who are over burdened with countless sorrows.

Bharata bhūmiyil āyiram āyiram
jñānikal janmam eṭuttu
manvantaraṅgalkkum appuram māmuni
sattamar kaṇda tatvaṅgal

Thousands and thousands of Yogis have taken birth in the land of Bharat (India) and have lived these principles visualized by the great Sages of the ancient past.

Marttya lōkattinte dukham akattuvān
etrayō nagna satyaṅgal
pōrikennōmalē jōli nirtti nī
entētu tanne yennennum

To remove the sorrows of humanity there are profound truths. "My darling child, leaving all other works; come to Me, you are always Mine."

ANANTA RŪPIṆI

Ananta rūpiṇi ananta guṇavati
ananta nāmini girijē mā

O You with endless forms, infinite qualities, countless names, O Mother Girija.

Jagajananī trilōka pālini
viśva suvāsini śubhadē mā
durmmati nāśini sanmatidāyini
bhōga mōkṣa sukha kāriṇi mā

You are the Mother sustaining the three worlds. Auspiciously married one, You are my Mother, do bless me. You grace the world with auspiciousness and bestow happiness on all, the worldly and the spiritually minded.

Paramē pārvvatī sundari bhagavatī
durgē bhāmati tvam mē mā
prasīda mātar nagēndra nandini
cira sukha dāyini jayadē mā

O embodiment of the supreme, daughter of the Himalayas, beautiful one, You are Bhagavati, the fierce Durga and my Mother. Bless me, Mother, You who are the bliss of Siva. You bestow ever-lasting happiness, O victorious one, my Mother.

ANBĀṬIKKAṆṆANTE PĀDAṄGAL

Anbāṭikkaṇṇante pādaṅgal
puṇarum poncilanbāyenkil
tṛkkarattāriṇa puṇarnnu ninnīṭunna
ponnōṭakkuzhalāyenkil kaṇṇā

If only I could be the golden anklets embracing the feet of Krishna of Ambadi. If only I could be the golden flute caressing the palms of Your hand, O Kanna.

Nin narumpuñcirittēn nukarnnīṭunna
madhubhṛ gamāyenkil
janmaśataṅgal nīntikkaṭannente
jīvitam dhanyamāyēnē kaṇṇā

If only I could be the honey bee tasting the sweet honey of Your soft smile, my life would be blessed - bypassing thousands of births.

Nin cāru rūpam ninachu ninachival
sarvam maraṇirunnenkil
añjali kūppi ñān tozhutu vilikkunnu
dēvā kanivarulū kaṇṇā kanivarulū

If only I could forget everything by constantly remembering Your beautiful form. With folded hands I cry for You - O Deva, have mercy! O Kanna, have mercy!

ĀSŪ BHARĒ

Āsū bharē nayanōm sē
pūchē rādhā śyām sē
rādhē śyām ō rādhē śyām
kyō ham kō chōḍ gayē

With tear-filled eyes, Radha asks Sri Krishna, "O Radhe Syam, why did You leave us and go away?"

Kucha kēhakar nahi gayē
na sandēsa vō dē gayē
muḍkar bhi nā dēkh gayē
anāth ham tō hō gayē
rādhē śyām ō rādhē śyām

He left without saying a word, neither did He leave us a message of consolation, nor did He look back even once. Alas, we have become orphans without Him.

Sapnā hē sach nahi
kānhā itnē kaṭōr nahi
kehatā hē man yē mērā
yahā kahi vō chip gayē
rādhē śyām ō rādhē śyām

This is just a dream; it cannot be true. Krishna is not stone-hearted to this extent. My mind tells me that surely Sri Krishna must be hiding somewhere nearby.

Tū na āyā to sunalē śyām
asuvan ki jamunā bahēgi
dūbēgi yē vṛndāvan
rādhā phir kabhi nahi milēgi
rādhē śyām ō rādhē śyām

If You will not return, O Lord, my tears will flow like the river Yamuna, and the whole of Vrindavan will be submerged in the river of grief. Then, You will never again see Your beloved Radha.

Tujē mērī kasam ājāvō śyām
ham par dhōḍi dayā karō
prāṇa nāthā tum hi hō sahārā

ham par dhōḍi kṛpā karō

Please promise me, O Lord, that You will come. Please show a little compassion. You alone are our support in this life. Shower at least a little of Your grace upon us.

ATI ĀNANDA DĒ

Ati ānanda dē paramānanda dē
tērē nāmkā guṇ gān
jay rām jay rām jay śrī rām
raghupati rāghava rājā rām

O Rama, glory to You, what a supreme bliss it is to sing Your divine name.

Jay jay rām rām rām sita rām
jay jay rām rām rām sita rām

Victory to Lord Rama!

Dō akṣarōm kā nām tērā
mahimā uski śabdō kē pār
pāpōm ka bhār kṣaṇ mē miṭhē
jō bhajē jay śrī rām

Your blessed name has just two syllables but Your greatness is beyond words. The burden of sins is removed for those who chant the name "Ram."

Man mē jis kē guñcē rām
vahi prabhu kā mangala dām
man mē jiskē dāskā bhāv
vahi viśrām karttē rām

The glorious Lord resides in one whose inner realm resonates with the word "Ram." The Lord rests in the heart of one who is humbler than the humblest.

Japu sadāmē nām tērā
ēsā var mē māngu rām
divya rūp kā daras dēkar
tumsē ēk kar dō rām

May I chant Your name always, Lord Ram. Let the desire to chant grow stronger in me. By granting me the glorious vision of Your form, please make me one with You.

ĀYĪ HĒ HŌLI

Āyī hē hōli bhari pichkkāri
śyām na āyē hōli nā manāyi

The festival of Holi (the Indian festival of colors) has come. The water piston is full with watercolor. But Shyam has not arrived. How can we celebrate without Him?

Ranga nahi tan rē
rang gayā hē man
virah ki rang tūnē
ham par lagāyi

The body is not smeared with color, but our minds are, for You have applied the color of grief (of separation) to our hearts.

Mōrē śyām hamrē sang khēlō hōli
rāh dēkhē tērē nit ham kṛṣṇā kṛṣṇā śrī kṛṣṇā

O Shyam, come and play Holi with us. We are eagerly waiting for You, Sri Krishna.

Bhīg gayā hē tan
khēlē bin hōli
bēhat hē asuvan
daras ko mōhan

The body has become wet even without spraying the colored water. How is it so? It is because of the tears we have shed awaiting Your darshan.

Kōyi tō samjhāyē usē
kōyi tō lē āyē
vraj ki yād usē
kōyi tō dilāyē

O, will someone make Him understand our pathetic condition. Please bring Him to us. At least kindle the remembrance of Vrindavan in His heart.

BHAGAVĀN KṚṢṆĀ ĀKAR

Bhagavān kṛṣṇā ākar muralī madhura bajādē
muralī madhura bajādē

O Lord Krishna, come play Your sweet flute!

Gitā kā divya gānā
vē bhavya bhāvanāyēm
gākar hamēm sunādē
sundar svarōm mē phirsē

With Your melodious voice, sing to us again the divine song of the Gita. Sing to us of those beautiful ideals.

Kṛṣṇā kṛṣṇā giridhārī
kṛṣṇā kṛṣṇā vanamālī
kṛṣṇā kṛṣṇā danujārī

O Krishna, who raised the Govardhana mountain, Krishna, who wears a garland of forest flowers, O my Lord, enemy of the demons!

Parivār viṣva sārā
hē prāṇimātra pyārā
ēkātmatā kē mōhan
mṛdu mantra kō sunādē

The universe is Your family, every creature Your beloved. Please grant us that vision of oneness.

Niṣkāma karma karanā
lōgōm kē dukha haranā
is karma yōga path kō
phir sē hamēm sikhādē

Work selflessly to remove people's suffering and teach us once again the ideals of karma yoga.

BHAKTI DĒ MĀ

Bhakti dē mā (2x)
dē mā bhakti
bhakti dē mā

Divine Mother, please bestow devotion.

Dāna yahī basa tujhasē māngū
prēma bhakti tum dēnā mā
prēma bhakti tum dēnā mā

This is the boon that I ask of You, O Mother, bless me with supreme devotion.

Mōha rāga sab dūr karō mā
chain tū man kī dēnā mā
divya prēma sē mujhkō bhar dē
man nirmala kara dē mā
man nirmala kara dē mā

Remove all delusion and attachment and grant me peace of mind. Fill my heart with divine love and thus purify it.

Dvāra tērī mē āyā hū maiyā
śaraṇa mē mujhkō lē lō mā
bhaṭakē nā man aur kahī mā
tujhmē līna rahē mā
tujhmē līna rahē mā

O Mother, I have come to Your doorstep, grant me refuge. Let all the wanderings of my mind cease and let it remain ever fixed upon You.

BHAVĀNI JAGADAMBĒ

Bhavāni jagadambē
gaṇēṣa guhamātē
himādritanayē mā
kṛpārdra hṛdayē mā

O Bhavani, the companion of Shiva, the universal Mother, Mother of Ganesh and Guha, daughter of the Himalayan Mountains, Your heart is melting with compassion.

Sarōja dalanētrī
suramyaśubha gātrī
trivarga phaladātrī
bhavārti bhayahantrī

Lotus-eyed Mother, embodiment of beauty and auspiciousness, You dispense the results of actions that are done in any of the three worlds. You destroy the fear of the sorrowful cycle of transmigration.

Manōjña guṇaṣīlē
mahēśī harajāyē
munīndra natapādē
vidhindra harivandyē

O embodiment of noble qualities, friend of Shiva, Your sacred feet are saluted by Sages, Brahma, Indra and Vishnu.

Kavīndranuta kīrtē
vinōdadhṛta mūrttē
kadamba vanasamsthē
samasta hṛdayasthē

O Mother, You are glorified by all poets; You have assumed a form as if for play. Though You reside in the forest of kadamba trees, in essence You are the indweller in the hearts of all.

BŌLŌ BŌLŌ GŌKULA BĀLĀ

Bōlō bōlō gōkula bālā
gōpālā jay gōpālā
bōlō bōlō nanda kumārā
gōpālā jay gōpālā

Sing, sing to the cowherd boy of Vrindavan, victory to the son of Nanda.

Nanda kumārā navanita cōrā
vṛndāvana sañcārī
yadukula nāyaka gōpakumārā
yamunā tīra vihārī

O descendant of Nanda, butter thief, who roams throughout Vrindavan, the Lord of the Yadus, son of a cowherd, You wander along the banks of the Yamuna river.

Kanmaṣanāśana hē madhusūdana
karunāmaya kamsārē
nitya nirāmaya bhava bhaya mōcaka
pāpa vimōcana kṛṣṇā [deva]

You destroy all sins and You destroyed the demon, Madhu. O compassionate one, eternal one, devoid of sorrows, liberated from samsara, You are our only refuge.

CHŌṬĪ CHŌṬĪ GAIYĀ

Chōṭī chōṭī gaiyā chōṭē chōṭē gvāl
chōṭō sō mērō madana gōpāl

A herd of little cows and a group of little cowherd boys, my enchanting little Gopal is with them.

Ghās khāvē gaiyā dūdh pīvē gvāl
mākhan khāvē mērō madana gōpāl

The cows eat the grass, the cowherd boys drink the milk and my little Gopal eats the butter.

Āgē āgē gaiyā pīchē pīchē gvāl
bīch mēm mērō madana gōpāl

The cows go in front, the little cowherds come behind and my little Gopal is in the middle.

Chōṭī chōṭī lakuṭi chōṭē chōṭē hāth
bansī bajāvē mērō madana gōpāl

Little pieces of sticks in their small pairs of hands, my enchanting Gopal plays the flute.

Chōṭī chōṭī sakhiyām madhuban bāl
rās rachāvē mērō madana gōpāl

Little female companions and the boy of Vrindavan, my little Gopal enchants everyone with His divine drama.

CINTANAI CEYTIṬUVĀY

Cintanai ceytiṭuvāy manamē
hariyin tirunāmam
dinam vandanai ceytiṭuvāy manamē
vallalin porpādam

O mind, think of Lord Hari's divine name and prostrate at the blessed feet of that ocean of compassion.

Āśaiyin piṭitanilē nīyum
allal kolkinṭrāy
ānandavaṭivinai ādisvarūpanai
arindiṭa marukinṭrāy

You are falling into trouble, trapped in the hands of desires, yet you refuse to know the blissful, eternal Lord.

Māyaiyām ulakinilē nīyum
mayanki nirkinṭrāy
maraikalil ōtiṭum māśilā oliyai
marande pōkindrai

You forget yourself in this world of maya. You have forgotten the untainted, supreme light within yourself that the Vedas are glorifying.

Hari ōm hari ōm

DARŚAN KI ICHĀ HĒ TŌ

Darśan ki ichā hē tō
durgā durgā bōl
ambā ambā bōl mātā
ambā ambā bōl

If you have the desire for liberation, chant the name, "Durga," sing the name, "Mother!"

Ambā ambā bōl jay jay
durgā durgā bōl

Chant, "Mother," chant, "Durga." Victory to Durga and the Mother.

Bhakti bhāv milnā hē tō
śakti śakti bōl
kālī kālī bōl mātā kālī śakti bōl
kālī kālī bōl jay jay śakti śakti bōl

If you want devotion to the Lord, chant the name, "Sakti." Sing, "Kali, Mother, Sakti!" Victory to Kali, victory to Sakti.

Ōm śaktī ōm śaktī ōm
kālī kālī jay jay jay
durgā durgā jay jay jay
ambā ambā jay jay jay

Victory to Kali, Durga and the Mother.

DĒVI ŚARAṆAM DURGE ŚARAṆAM

Dēvi śaraṇam durgē śaraṇam
kālī śaraṇam lakṣmī śaraṇam
śaraṇam śaraṇam śaraṇam śaraṇam
śaraṇam jagadambā śaraṇam jagadambā

O Devi, I take refuge in You. O Durga, give me Your protection! O Kali, supreme refuge, O Lakshmi, protect me. Universal Mother, protect me! Universal Mother, protect me!

Amalē vimalē karuṇānilayē
kamalē kalayē kalimalaśamanē
śivaramaṇi guhajananī mahitē
śaraṇam jagadambā

O pure one, immaculate one, reservoir of compassion, Goddess Lakshmi, sweet one, destroyer of the impurities of the Kali Yuga, Lord Shiva's beloved consort, Mother of Lord Guha, O great one who is adored, I take refuge in You - O Goddess of the universe.

Śubhadē sukhadē śivapadanilayē
girijē vanajē girirājasutē
śubhavaradē śritajananī sumukhī
śaraṇam jagadambā

O bestower of well being, giver of happiness, who is rooted in the sacred scriptures, who was born out of the mountain, who was born in the forest, O daughter of the king of the mountains, who grants us the boon of auspiciousness, Mother of all who take refuge in You, O Mother with a beautiful face, I take refuge in You - O Mother of the universe.

Rasikē ramaṇī ripukula bhayadē
lasitē lalitē śrutipadanilayē
smaraṇam satatam tava padakamalam
śaraṇam jagadambā

O delightful one, beautiful one, who creates fear in the enemy, O playful one, gentle one, whose feet are rooted in the Vedas, constantly I remember Your lotus feet - O Mother of the universe, I take refuge in You.

DĪNA JANA DUKHA HĀRIṆI AMMĒ

Dīna jana dukha hāriṇi ammē
karunā rasa vāhiṇi amme amṛtanandamayi
maruvuka mānasamalaril
coriyuka snēhamṛta madhuram

O Mother, You are the destroyer of the sorrows of the afflicted and the giver of the nectar of compassion. Always remain in the flower of my mind and shower the sweet nectar of Your eternal love.

Viraham mama hṛdi vēdanayenkilum
smaraṇayatonnē mama jīvanam
orunāl ninnil aliyānariyāte
akatār satatam viṅgukayāyi amṛteśvari

My heart suffers from the pain of separation. It is only by remembering You that I am able to stay alive. My heart weeps constantly to merge one day with You.

Tapta manassinu taṇalēkiṭum
karuṇāmalar viriyum taru nī
ārilumoruvidha bhēdavumillāte
āvōlam nī kṛpa coriyum amṛteśvari

Mother, You are a tree that gives cool shade to burning hearts, a tree full of blossoms of compassion. You shower Your grace generously on everyone without any distinctions of any kind.

Āśrayamattoru jīvaneyennum
snēhōṣmalamāy tazhukiṭum
mṛdu pavanōpama tava kṛpayāl tiru
caraṇaṅgalilāy cēkuka nī amṛteśvari

Lovingly You embrace this soul that is burdened by countless desires. With the gentle breeze of Your grace, allow me, as well, to reach Your holy feet.

Amṛta rasōtbhava tava vacassālī
yazhlil tāpamakattuka nī
amṛtēśvarī nī aviratam en hṛdi
amṛtānandam melkīṭumō

Kindly remove my sorrow with Your sweet words! O immortal Goddess, will You step into my heart with Your lotus feet?

DĪNA NĀTHĒ

Dīna nāthē dīna vatsalē
dīnata tīrkkum dīna dayāmayī

You are the guardian and the consolation of the suffering masses, O compassionate one; You remove our sorrows.

Vannīṭumō hṛdayattilammē
varuvān iniyum tāmasamō

Won't You come to my heart? Why do You delay in coming?

Kēṇu kēṇu karaññu vilichu
kēlkkunnillē ammē varikayillē

Don't You hear the constant, loud cry of this child? Mother, won't You come?

Kēlkunna nālini eṇṇuvānāy
ottoru śaktiyum illayammē

I have no strength left to wait for that day when You will hear my heart felt cry.

ĒK DIN KĀLI MĀ

Ēk din kāli mā
ānḍē dil mē āyēgi
diyē jagamagāyōmgē
divāli hō jāyēgi

Some day, Mother Kali will come into the darkness of my heart. Lamps will illumine and sparkle, and it will become the festival of lights (Diwali.)

Divya jyōti varṣā mē
prakṛti bhi harṣāyēgī
har diśā kī ōr sē
ōmkār dhvani gūmjēgī

In that shower of divine radiance, all of nature will spontaneously rejoice. From every direction, the divine sound of "Om" will reverberate.

Gūmjēgī ōm gūmjēgī ōm ōm
ōmkār dhvani gūmjēgī

Again and again, the sound of "Om" will resound.

Man kā mōn nācēgā
mast mē mō jāvūmgī
pamgha bin uṭ jāvumgī
ākāś mē ban jāvūmgī

The peacock of my mind will dance and I will become ecstatic. Even without wings I will fly. I will become the vast, expansive sky.

ELLĀMIRIKKILUM

Ellāmirikkilum illātirikkil nī
vallāyma jīvitam entammē
ellām tikaññoren vīṭum kinākkalum
pūnilāvillātta rātri ammē

Though I may possess everything, my life is miserable in Your absence. My house, with all of its comforts, and all of my dreams, are like a dark night that is devoid of moonlight.

Neyvilakkāyiram katti ninnīṭilum
kuriruṭṭeṅgumē enteyammē
pūkāvanaṅgalō pūttulaññīṭilum
pūmaṇamilla nirappakiṭṭum

Even if a thousand lamps are filled with ghee and lit, I behold only darkness. Though I may behold gardens filled with flowers, I experience neither their fragrance nor their colorful appearance.

Āṭakal ābharaṇaṅgal aṇiññoru
nirjjīva dēhaminnen janmam
ammayāmātmāvuṇarnnu cirikkātta
janmamitentoru janmam ammē

My life has become like that of a corpse wearing beautiful garments and ornaments. Of what purpose is this life if You, Mother, the soul, do not awaken laughing?

Ninpāda pūjayil ente niśvāsaṅgal
ente viśvāsaṅgal dhanyamākān
nīyām viśuddhiyil ennātma cumbanam
nirvṛti pūkān tuṇaykum ammē

May my breath and my faith generate blessings through the worship of Your holy feet. Mother, please help me to experience bliss by merging in You, the embodiment of purity.

ENAIKKĀKKA UNAIYANṬRI

Enaikkākka unaiyanṭri tuṇaiyārammā en
vinaitīrkka nīyanṭri gati ētammā
nānundan padam kiṭakkum sēyallavō nī
anpennum pāluṭṭum tāyallavō

O my Mother, but for You, there is no one to grant me refuge, no one to remove my sorrows. Am I not but a small child at Your feet? Are You not my affectionate Mother feeding me with the milk of love?

Aṭittālum aṇaittālum nīyē annai uyir
muṭindālum piriyēn tiruppādam tannai
eṭuttennai anaittuntan arul kāṭṭuvay
ennālum unai maravā nilai kūṭṭuvāy

Whether You beat me or embrace me, still, You are my Mother. Even in death I will cling to Your blessed feet. Please take me in Your arms, hold me tightly and bless me. May the remembrance of You never leave me.

Azhukinṭra kaṇkalai nī kāṇātatēn
anpōṭu ōṭi vandu anaikkātatēn
ārutalāy oru sollai kūrātatēn
aṭiyavarkal tuyar tanaiyum tīrkkātatēn

Can You not see my tear filled eyes? Why don't You come and caress me? Why do You not soothe me with Your consoling words? O Mother, won't You remove my sorrows?

EṄGUM UN ARUL MAZHAIYĒ

Ēṅgum un arul mazhaiyē
poṅgum kaṭal alai pōlē
perukiṭumē śānti
tāyē un sannidiyil

O Mother, Your grace is overflowing like the waves of the sea. In Your divine presence peace prevails.

Aṅjukindra en manadin
tañjam untan tāy maḍiyē
anbozhugum pēchil tuyar
pañju pōla parantiṭum

Your lap is the only refuge for this child's frightened mind. When I hear Your soothing words, sorrows fly away like cotton in the wind.

Vañja millā manam camaithu
mañja mena atai amaitēn
keñji keñji unai azhaittēn
koñja matil vantamarvāy

I am calling again and again, crying for a glimpse of You in my mind. Let this innocence purify my mind and make it an abode for You. I am calling You again and again to come and dwell there.

Solvatellām tiru mantiram āgavum
ceyvatellām untan tiruppaṇi āgavum
kēṭpatellām untan kani mozhi āgavum
kaniṅtarul purinteṇṇai kaṭaitēdra vārāy

Please bestow Your grace upon me so that whatever words I speak may become Your mantra, whatever I do may become Your work and whatever I hear may be Your kind words. Thus take me across this ocean of transmigration.

amṛtēśvarī namo namah
bhuvanēśvarī namo namah
jagadiśvarī namo namah
sarvēśvarī namo namah

ENNULLIL MINNUNNA

Ennullil minnunna ninniluṇarunna
eṅgum niraññoru daivam (2x)
prēmattin mantram pozhiykkunna daivam
snēhattin cuṭumuttam pakarunna daivam
ammayāy vannu innende daivam
dīnānukanpatan pūrṇṇakumbham ammē ammē

The God who shines inside of me, who is awake inside of you, who fills everything in this world, the God who chants the mantra of love and bestows warm, affectionate kisses, the vessel full to the brim with compassion, O Mother, Mother, Mother.

Akaleyāṇeṅkillum kāruṇyavāridhi
ariyunnu nī ente saṅkaṭaṅgal
kanivāla kattunnu durghaṭaṅgal
ariyāte ceytōraparādhavāridhiyil
alayāte tīramaṇāchiṭunnu
ā alivil ñān tanne aliñjiḍunnu ammē ammē

O ocean of compassion, even when You are far away You know my sorrows. Out of compassion, You remove the obstacles that I face. Not leaving me to struggle in the ocean of sins committed unknowingly, You take me to the other shore.

Janmāntaraṅgalāy ceytatām pāpattin
phalaminnennē cuzhattiṭunnu ghōra
vipinattilennē āzhttiṭunnu
vīṇṭumī jīvitam pūvaṇiyāninnēkamām
pōmvazhi śaraṇāgati
snēhaswarūpattil bāṣpāñjali
ammē nīyegati ammē

The consequences of sins committed during many lifetimes torment me now, throwing me into the depths of a terrible forest. For my life to flower once again, I must surrender totally to You, the embodiment of love, to worship Your form with my tears.

GAṆANĀTHĀ ŌM GAṆANĀTHĀ

Gaṇanāthā ōm gaṇanāthā
ōm sidhi vināyaka gaṇanāthā

O Lord of the Ganas (Ganapati), greatest of the siddhis.

Praṇava śarīrā prapanna śaraṇā
pārvatī putrā parāt parā
gaṇapati dēvā gajamukha ramyā
guruguhavandyā śivātmajā

Your body is the pranava mantra; Your grace flows to Your devotees, O son of Goddess Parvati, subtler than the subtlest, Lord Ganapati with the head of an elephant, the enchanter, worshipped by Subramanyan, son of Shiva.

Cāru śarīrā candana varṇṇā
cāmara karṇṇā cidātmakā
śōbhana rūpa śamkara tanaya
sidhida varadā dayā mayā

Your charming body with flapping ears is the color of sandalwood. O essence of knowledge, endowed with a radiant form, the son of Shiva, bestowing powers and boons, O embodiment of compassion.

Sādhaka sūkhadā mōhanacaritā
mrityu janma hara ganēśvara
vighna gaṇāntaka viśva manōhara
vēda vihāraṇā vināyaka

Your presence inspires joy in the devotees. Your deeds are exciting. Birth and death are powerless before You, Lord of Ganas. You obliterate all obstacles and mesmerize the entire universe. Your secret lies in the Vedas.

GARUDHA VĀHANĀ

Garudha vāhanā kṛṣṇā gōpi mādhavā
vijaya mōhanā kṛṣṇā janmakōmalā
nayanamōhanā kṛṣṇā nīlaśarirā
mādhavā harē kṛṣṇā sundarakṛtē

Krishna, Your vehicle is the great bird named Garuda, O enchanter, ever-beautiful one, You are soothing to the eyes, O Krishna of dark hue.

Kamala lōcanā kṛṣṇā kāruṇārupā
kadana nāśanā kṛṣṇā kamsamardana
caraṇa pallavam kṛṣṇā taruṇakōmalam
tāvaka nāmam kṛṣṇā mōkṣadāyakam

Your eyes resemble lotus petals, O Krishna, You are the embodiment of compassion. Krishna, Your tender feet are enchanting, the constant repetition of Your divine name grants one liberation.

Harē rāma harē rāma rāma rāma harē harē
harē kṛṣṇā harē kṛṣṇā kṛṣṇā kṛṣṇā harē harē

GĀŪ RĒ TUJHĒ ABHANGA

Harī sadā vasē tatra yatra bhāgavatā nāḥ
gāyanti bhakti bhāvēna harē nāmaiva kēvalam
jaya hari viṭṭhala viṭṭhala pānduranga
jaya hari viṭṭhala viṭṭhala pānduranga

The Lord always looks after those who remember Him and sing His praises with devotion. Salutations to Lord Vithala, the Lord of Pandharpur.

Gāū rē tujhē abhanga
jay jay viṭṭhala pānduranga
hē dēvā tujhā sūṭē na sanga
dharuna ghē malā pānduranga
dharuna ghē malā pānduranga
gāū rē tujhē abhanga
jay jay viṭṭhala pānduranga

We are singing Your abhangas (traditional and devotional chants of Maharashtra), O Lord Vithala. May Your divine presence always be with us wherever we go. Embrace me in Your arms, O Panduranga.

Jay hari viṭṭhala pānduranga
gāū rē tujhē abhanga (gāū rē tujhē)

Salutations to Lord Vithala, the Lord of Pandharpur, we are singing Your abhangas.

Jīva mājhā phasalā asā
samsāra pāra karu mī kasā

kṛpā tujhī hī āśā mājhī
nakō rē nakō rē malā sukha samsārāchī

My life is caught in the ocean of samsara, how do I cross it? Your grace is my only hope. I do not desire for any pleasures of the world.

Mānavācī samaj aśī
ghara sampatti hī kharōkharī
ēka divas tō sōḍūn jātō
pakaḍūn pakaḍūn yam tyālā ghē ūn jātō

Man is so foolish to think that his house and wealth will remain with him forever. One day he has to leave them and go, being snatched away by the Lord of death.

Bhajana mhaṇu ati premānē
śuddha karū mana tujhyā nāmānē
tujhyā caranī ālō mī dēvā
śubhadāyaka śubhadāyaka
kara hē jīvana mājhē

O Lord, I sing Your bhajans with love and devotion. I try to purify my heart chanting Your divine name. I have sought refuge at Your lotus feet. Please make this life auspicious and grant me true fulfilment.

Jaya jaya viṭṭhala jaya hari viṭṭhala

Salutations to Lord Vithala.

GĪT NAHĪ

Gīt nahī sur nahī phir bhi mē gāvūm
tū hī batā mērī mā mē kyā karūm

I don't have a song and I don't have a melody, but still I sing. O Mother, won't You tell me what else can I do?

Kitanē janmō sē tujhē ḍhūnḍ rahā hum
tērē caraṇō kī rāh mē nahī jānu
śakti nahī rāstā nahī phir bhī mē khōjūm
tū hī batā mērī mā mē kyā karūm

For how many births have I been searching for You? I don't know the way to Your holy feet. I don't have the strength and I don't know the path, but still I search for You. O Mother, won't You tell me what else can I do?

Pāpō kā bōjhā uṭhāyē bhaṭak rahā hum
mērē dil kā phul tō murajhā gayā hē
śuddhi nahī puṣpa nahī phir bhi mē pūjūm
tū hī batā mērī mā kyā karūm

Carrying my burden of sins I wander aimlessly; the flower of my heart has wilted. I am not pure and I don't have any flowers, but still I worship You. O Mother, won't You tell me what else can I do?

Mērē dil mē tērē liyē kitane gīta hē
likhanē vālā gānā vālā kahām sē āyē
gīt nahī sur nahī phir bhi mē gāvum
tū hī batā mērī mā mē kyā karūm

So many songs for You are in my heart, but I am neither a poet nor a singer. I don't have a song and I don't have a melody, but still I sing. O Mother, won't You tell me what else can I do?

GŌVIṆDA GŌPĀLĀ HARI HARI

Gōviṇda gōpālā hari hari
gōviṇda gōpālā
gāvō gāvō hari guṇa gāvō
jaya hari jaya hari gōpālā

Victory to the Lord and protector of the cows, to the destroyer of sins. Sing the glories of the Lord.

Mādhava gōpālā hari hari
mōhana gōpālā
prēma sē bōlō sab mil bōlō
jaya hari jaya hari gōpālā

Victory to the companion of Lakshmi, enchanting cowherd boy. Let everybody sing together with love and joy. Victory to the Lord.

Madhura madhura hē madhura madhura
tērā nām gōpālā
prēma sē bōlō sab mil bōlō
jaya hari jaya hari gōpālā

Salutations to the friend of Lakshmi, enchanting cowherd boy. Your name is the sweetest name of all.

gōviṇda hari hari gōpālā hari har

GURU CARAṆAM GURU

Guru caraṇam guru caraṇam
śrī guru caraṇam bhava haraṇam
parama guru caraṇam bhava haraṇam
sat guru caraṇam bhava haraṇam

Salutations to the powerful, eternal feet of the Guru that free us from worldliness.

Amṛtānandamayī guru caraṇam
papa vimōciṇi guru caraṇam
guru caraṇam guru caraṇam
sat guru caraṇam bhava haraṇam

The feet of the Guru Mata Amritanandamayi release us from all sins. Salutations to the eternal feet of the Guru that free us from worldliness.

Guru mahārāṇī guru mahārāṇī
guru dēvō sat guru mahārāṇī
guru braḥma guru viṣṇu guru mahārānī
guru dēvō mahēśvara guru mahārānī

The Guru is the Empress, the Guru is God, the Guru is Brahma, Vishnu and Siva.

GURU KṚPĀ DṚṢṬI

Gūmga śabdōm sē gūmj uṭhē
lamgḍā bhī parvat pār karē
kṛpā dṛṣṭi sē tērē hē satgurō
amṛtēśvaryai namō namaḥ

When Your grace flows through Your glance, O Satguru, the dumb will resonate with words and the lame will be able to climb even the mountains. Prostrations to Amriteshvari, the immortal Goddess.

Guru kṛpā dṛṣṭi sē pāvan mē hō gayī
bhāvarī bhāvarī bhāvarisī hō gayī
karuṇā bharī ākhōm kē sāgara mē khō gayī
karuṇā bharī amṛtamayī sāgara mē khō gayī
hōś āyī śīś jhukī mē tō vahīm rō paḍī

The glance of grace of the Guru has purified me. From that experience I have become like one gone mad. I have sunk into the vast ocean of the infinite compassion of those radiant eyes, that nectarous, overflowing compassion. Regaining my senses, with my head bowed low in reverence, I helplessly burst into tears.

**Guru divya dṛṣṭi sē prakāśīt mē hō gayī
sāvalī sāvalī sāvalī sī ramga gayī
apār jis kaṭākṣ kō mē yug yug taras gayī
yug yug taras gayī śat yug taras gayī
pakē usē gad gad mē tō vahīm hams paḍi**

The divine glance of the Guru has enlightened me. I have become as if camouflaged with that dark complexion. For this unlimited destiny I have longed for eons. I have been longing for eons, for hundreds of eons. On achieving it, I am overcome with joy; immediately I burst out laughing.

HARA HARA MAHĀDĒVĀ ŚAMBHŌ

**Hara hara mahādēvā śambhō
kaśi viśvanātha gaṅgē**

O great God Shiva, Lord of Benares, Lord of the Ganga, Lord of the universe.

**Kaśi viśvanātha gaṅgē
kaśi amarnātha gaṅgē**

Lord of Benares, Lord of the Ganges, Lord of Amarnatha, Lord of the universe.

**Hara hara mahādēvā śambhō
kaśi viśvanātha gaṅgē**

HĒ MĀDHAVĀ MADHUSŪDHANA

**Hē mādhavā madhusūdhana
dayā karō hē yadu nandala**

O Krishna, beloved of Lakshmi, the slayer of the demon, Madhu; compassionate one, born in the clan of Yadu.

Hē yādavā muralīdhara
śyāma gōpālā giridhārabālā

Belonging to the Yadu clan, holding the flute, dark-coloured one, lifting the mountain Giridhara.

Nanda nandana gōvinda
navanita cōra gōvinda
mathura nāthā gōvinda
muralī manōhara gōvinda

Son of Nanda, Lord of the cows, stealer of butter, Lord of Mathura, the enchanting player of the flute.

Gōvinda gōvinda rādhē śyāma gōvinda
nanda kumāra gōvinda navanita cōra gōpālā

Lord of the cows, dark-coloured one, cowherd boy, the son of Nanda, the stealer of butter.

IṢWAR TUMHI DAYĀKARŌ

Iṣwar tumhi dayākarō
tum bin hamāra kaun hai

O Lord, please show us mercy. Other than You, who is here to look after us?

Jag kō racanē wala tu
jag kō mitanē wala tu
bigdi bananē wala tu
tum bin hamāra kaun hai

You are the creator and the destroyer of the world. Even misfortune is Your creation. Other than You, who is here for us?

Mātā tumhi tumhi pīṭā
bandhu tumhi tumhi sakhā

kēval tumhāra āsra
tum bin hamāra kaun hai

You are our Mother, Father, Benefactor and Friend. You are our only refuge. Other than You, who is here for us?

Kuch bhi nahin hamēn khabar
tērī lagan kō chōḍa kar
jāyēn tō jāyē hum kidhar
tum bin hamāra kaun hai

We don't know anything. Without our love for You, what would become of us? Other than You, who is here for us?

JĀGŌ MĀ KĀLI JĀGŌ JĀGŌ

Jāgō mā kāli jāgō jāgō
jāgō mā śyāmā jāgō jāgō

Wake up, rise up, Mother Kali; wake up Mother Shyama, the blue-coloured one.

Ā khaḍē hē yahā par yē duśman sabhī
kāma mada lōbha kuch hē nāma unkē
lē jāyēngē mā mujhkō baṇākē kaidī
kāli tērī jhalak sē miṭ jāyēngē sabhī

The powerful enemies known as lust, pride and greed are overpowering me; they will carry me away and imprison me. O Mother Kali, if You merely glance at me then they will all be destroyed.

Tū na āyē tō maiyā kahēngē sabhī
iskī māmē thoḍī sī dayā hī nahī
rōtā hē yē śiśu par bhī mā hē sōyī
karō rakṣā mērī jāgō mā tum abhī

If You do not come, then all will say that my Mother has no compassion at all. This child of Yours is crying, are You fast asleep? Save me, Mother, rise up now!

JĀGŌ MĒRĒ PYĀRĒ BĀLĀ

Jāgō mērē pyārē bālā
nanhē naṭ khaṭ nandalālā
bār bār mēnē tujhē jagāyā
muḍ muḍ kē tu phir so gayā

Wake up my darling boy, O mischievous little son of Nanda. I wake You up again and again, but You turn around and go back to sleep.

Sūraj kī pahalī kiraṇē
tērē chēharē pē khēlē
mīṭhī mīṭhī bātē tērī
āngan mē koyal bōlē

The first rays of sunlight are playing on Your face. In the courtyard, the cuckoo bird is singing the sweet tales of Your divine deeds.

Dēkh tērī pyāri gāyē
van mē ghās caranē kō jāyē
tu nā uṭhā to mākhan cor
unkā dūdh ōr kōyi pī jāyē

Look, Your favorite cows are going to the forest to graze. If You don't get up, little butter thief, someone else will drink up all of their milk.

Sārē vraj kī kānha tūnē
kar dī hē dil kī cōrī

kuch tō kar ab khēl tamāśā
dikhā ham kō līlā tērī

O Kanna, You have stolen the heart of everyone in Vraj. Won't You play some mischief or make a drama and show us Your divine play?

JAHĀN DĒKHŪ

Jahān dēkhū vahā śyām tumi
sunti hu bas muralī dvani
kahti hu bas nām yahi
śyām hari mērē śyām hari

Everywhere I look, I find You. All that I hear is the sound of Your flute. And there is but one name on my lips, Shyam Hari, O my Shyam Hari.

Yād na āyē tujhkō mērī prabhu
aisē kyā kahō bhūl huyī
tarsē nayanā dars kō tērē
kab āvōgē śyām hari

What fault have I committed, O Lord, that has caused You to forget me? My eyes thirst for a glimpse of You. O, when will You come, my Shyam Hari?

Chōḍ gayē hō is tan kō prabhu
chōḍ na pāvōgē is man kō
rōm rōm mē kānhā tum hō
dil kī har dhaṭkan mē tumhi

Though You have left me physically, O Lord, You can never leave my mind. You are in every pore of my being, in each beat of my heart.

JAL RAHĀ HĒ

Jal rahā hē manavā mōrā
dō būnd ānsū dēnā mayyā
tērī yād mē nīr bahātā
ānsū nahī amṛt ban jātā

O Mother, my mind is burning. Please grant that I may shed two drops of tears. When I cry, remembering You, my tears become the nectar of bliss.

Jīvan kā hal khīncū mayā
sukh dukh cakra mē ghūmūn mātā
yē kyā huvā ab kyā hōgā
ēsi cintā mē ḍūbū mātā

I drag the heavy plow of life, O Mother, and I ride the wheel of joy and sorrow. I drown in overwhelming thoughts such as, "O, how could this have happened?" and, "What fate shall befall me now?"

Cintā kī agnī mē mayyā
kahīn mē pāgal nā ban jāvu
har cintā mērī tū hī jānē
kuch tō man kī śāntī dēdē

O Mother, let me not go mad in the burning fire of my thoughts and worries. You alone know my every thought, Mother. Please grant me at least some peace of mind.

Kis pē viśvās karūn mayyā
tērī śaraṇ mē āyā mātā
ānsūvō sē hō tērī pūjā
it nī kṛpā tō karnā mātā

Who else can I trust, Mother? I have come and taken refuge in You alone. Bestow at least a little grace on me so that I can perform Your worship with my tears.

JAYA DURGA DURGATI

Dēvi sarvabhūtēṣu śaktirūpēna samstita namastasyē namastasyē namastasyē namō namaḥ

To the Goddess, the soul of all beings in the universe, the embodiment of spiritual splendour, I humbly offer my sincere prostrations again and again.

Jaya durga durgati parihāriṇi
dukha vināsini mātāmṛitēṣwarī

Victory to Durga who removes all obstacles, who destroys all sorrows, O Mother, immortal Goddess.

Ādi śakti parabrahma swarūpiṇi
jagat jananī sarva vēda prakāṣiṇi
brahmā śiva hari archana ki mā
dhyāna karata sura nara muni jñāni

Primordial power, embodiment of the supreme Brahman, Mother of the universe, light of all the Vedas, even Brahma, Siva and Vishnu worship You. Gods, Sages and the enlightened ones meditate on You.

Bhakta pujātara rakta piyatē
simha savāra sakala varadāyiṇi
brahmānanda śaraṇamē āyō
bhava bhaya nāsaka amṛita swarūpiṇi

You are worshipped by Your devotees. You drink the essence of sacrifice. Mounted on a lion, bestowing boons, O bliss of Brahman, I take refuge in You. You destroy all the fear in the world, O embodiment of immortality.

JAYA JĀNAKIJĪVANA RĀMA

Jaya jānakijīvana rāma
smarakōḍi manōjña śarīrā
mithilāpati hṛdayanivāsā
munimānasa patmavihārā

Victory to Rama, the life of Janaki (Rama's wife, Sita Devi.) Remembrance to one with a body as handsome as a hundred thousand Gods. The Lord of the heart of Sita Devi, residing in the lotus of the hearts of the saints.

Jay jay rām sītā rām jay jay rām sītā rām
jay jay rām sītā rām jay jay rām(2x)

Victory to Sita and Rama

Bharatānana candra cakōrā
marutātmaja vanditapādā
dhṛtasāyaka cāpa manōjñā
daśakandhara darppa vināśā

You and Your brother Bharata are like a chakora bird and the moon. You are a brother to Hanuman, You carry the bow and arrow, O destroyer of the ten-headed Ravana, You have adorable feet.

Madhubhāṣaṇa mangala sadanā
patitāvana pāvana caraṇā
sukha sāgara sundara sumukhā
mṛduhāsa manōhara vadanā

Sweet-spoken, the abode of auspiciousness, saviour of the down-trodden, with purifying feet, the ocean of happiness, one with a most pleasing and beautiful form, with a sweet smile and an ever-handsome face.

Raghu vamśa śirō maṇi rāma
cira saukya vidhāyaka rāma
mṛti janma vimōcana rāma
jaya rāghava jānaki rāma

The adornment of the Raghu dynasty, O Rama, giver of happiness, who rescues us from the cycle of birth and death. Victory to Janaki's Lord, Rama of the Raghu dynasty.

JAY GAṆĒŚA JAY GAṆĒŚA

Jay gaṇēśa jay gaṇēśa jay gaṇēśa dēvā

Victory to Lord Ganesha.

Dīnōm kē dukha hartā tūm śānti pradātā
anātha kē nāth tūm
jay jay gaṇanāthā (2x)

O Lord Ganesha, the remover of the sorrows of the afflicted, granter of refuge and bestower of peace, victory unto You.

Lēkē nāma tērā prabhu
rakhē jō pahalā kadam
lakṣya kō vō pāvē dēvā
dūrhō uski aḍachan (2x)

O Lord, one who takes the first step on his path chanting Your name surely attains his goal and all the obstacles in his path disappear.

Śraddhā sē jō karē
tērā nit sumiran
ahamkār miṭ jāvē dēvā
pāvē bhakti mukti kā dhan (2x)

O Lord, one who remembers You daily with loving faith and attention has his ego destroyed. He thus gains the treasure of devotion and liberation.

Tava caraṇōm mē dēvā
arpit yē tan man
tērī kṛpā sē nāthā
ṭūṭē māyā kē banḍan (2x)

O Lord, I surrender this body and mind at Your holy feet. Your grace alone can liberate me from the bonds of delusion.

JAY HŌ HARĒ RĀM

Jay hō harē rām Jay hō harē rām
jay hō harē rām varada rāgava

Victory to Sri Ram, the bestower of boons.

Jō sabhī kē śaraṇa dāyaka
jin kē karōm mē dhanuṣa nāyaka

You grant refuge to all. O Rama, Your arms are adorned with a great bow and numerous arrows.

Śyām kalēbara patita pāvana
jay hō tērī āsura ghātaka

Rama, of a dark complexion, You are compassionate to ignorant sinners. Victory to You, O destroyer of evil.

Līlā tēri prēm pūrita
jīvan tērā tyāg pūrita

Your divine dramas are full of love, O Rama, and Your life is one of self sacrifice.

Nām tērā mantra tāraka
varadē hamē tū praṇat pālaka

Your divine name is the mantra that frees us from the cycle of birth and death. Rama, please bless us, You grant protection for the humble.

JAY JAGADAMBĒ JAY JAGADAMBĒ (JAG KĪ TṚṢṆĀ MIṬĀNĒ KŌ)

Jay jagadambē jay jagadambē jay jagadambē mā
jay jay mā jay jay mā jay amṛtēśvarī mā

Glory to the Mother of the universe, the immortal Goddess.

Jag kī tṛṣṇā miṭānē kō
prēmamayī tum āyī hō
jagajananī amṛtēṣvarī mām
karuṇā kī avatār hō

Mother of love, You have incarnated on this Earth to alleviate all of its sufferings. O Divine Mother, immortal Goddess, You are the embodiment of compassion.

Har lētī hō dukhō kā bhār
dētī hō mā śānti apār
karatī hō sab kō svīkār
jō āyē mā tērē dvār

You remove the burden of sorrows from Your children and thus bestow on them infinite peace. Your doors are never closed to anyone; You receive and accept all of those who come to You.

Jag kē sab tērī samtān
prēm tērā hai sabpē samān
tērī kṛpādṛṣṭi sē mā
pāpī banē kṣaṇ mē mahān

You look upon everyone in this world as Your own child. Your love is equal to all. Your compassionate glance alone is enough to transform a lost and sinful soul into a saint.

Pūrṇabrahma svarūpiṇī hō
satguru satyasanātanī hō
prēm bhakti samdāyinī hō
jananī tum śubhakāriṇī hō

You are the incarnation of the supreme Brahman. You are the true master, the eternal one and the Truth. You are the bestower of love and devotion. O Mother, You are the embodiment of auspiciousness.

JAY JAGADĪŚVARĪ

Jay jagadīśvarī mātā sarasvati
śaranāgata vrata pālana kāri
candra bimba sama vadana virājē
śaśimakuṭa mālā galadhāri

Victory to the Mother of the world, Sarasvati, whose face is as beautiful as the reflection of the moon, who vows to take care of Her devotees. Who wears the moon for a crown and a garland around Her neck.

Vīṇāvāma amgamē śōbhē
sāma gīta dhvani madhura pihāri
śvēta vasana kamalā sansundara

A veena rests beautifully on Your lap and sweet melodies emanate from You. In a white dress You sit in the beautiful lotus posture.

Samga sakhi śubhahāsa savāri
brahmānanda mē dās tumhārō
dē darśana parabrahma durāri

A swan is Your vehicle. You bring Your devotees to the highest bliss. Please appear before us, darling of the great Brahma.

JAY JAY DURGE

Jay jay durgē mātā bhavāni
sakala pūjitē vandē

Victory to Durga, Mother Bhavani, prostration to the one worshipped by all.

Darṣan dē dō kāli mātē
ēkbār phir sē
tujhē dēkhnē ki chāhat hē mā
man mērā rōyē

O Mother Kali, give me Your vision. My mind cries out ceaselessly desiring to see You.

Karuṇā kī tū sāgar hē mā
mujhkō tū har lē
tērī ēk jhalak hē kāphī
pāp mukti hōyē

You are the ocean of compassion. O Mother, save me. One glance from You is enough to save one from all sins.

JAY JAY SATGURU

Jay jay satguru maharāṇi amṛtānandamayī
jay jay durga maharāṇi amṛtānandamayī

Victory to the supreme Guru Amritanandamayi, the empress, who is a manifestation of Durga.

Amṛtēśvarī bhavāni
amṛtēśvarī śivāni
nārāyaṇi mama jananī
amba amṛtānandamayī

Immortal Goddess, You who are Bhavani, Siva and Narayani. My Mother, Mother Amritanandamayi.

Pūrṇṇa brahma swarūpiṇyai
satchidānanda mūrttayē
ātmārāmāgraganyāyai
amṛtēśvariyai namō namaḥ

The complete manifestation of Truth; existence, knowledge and bliss embodied; supreme among those revelling in the inner Self, prostrations to the immortal Goddess.

Sarvva mangala māmgalyē
śivē sarvartha sādhikē
śaraṇyē triyambakē gauri
nārāyaṇi namōstutē

You bestow auspiciousness, O consort of Siva, fulfiller of all desires, refuge of devotees, Gauri, Durga, prostrations to You.

Sudhāmayī dayāmayī
kṛpāmayī jaganmayī
surēśvarī mahēśvarī
śivamkarī abhayamkarī

Embodiment of purity, compassionate Mother, graceful one, Mother of all. You are the master of all Gods, O great Goddess, the wife of Siva and the bestower of fearlessness.

Suvāsini suhāsini

nitya brahmacāriṇi
yaśasvini tejasvini
sarvalōka pāvini

Auspiciously married one, having a beautiful smile, O eternal virgin, You bear all fame, luminous one, You sustain all the worlds.

JAY JAY ŚYĀMALA

Jay jay śyāmala sundari kāli
jay jay akhilōddhāriṇi kēli
ānandāmṛita varṣiṇi mahitē
kālātīta niṣēvaṇa niratē

Victory to Kali, the Goddess with a dark form. Victory to You who redeem the world. O great one, You grant immortal bliss. Even Shiva, the one who is beyond time, worships You.

Jaya bhayahāriṇi jaya bhavatāriṇi
amṛtapurēśvarī sundari kāli

Victory to the destroyer of fear, victory to the one who takes us across the ocean of transmigration.

Jay jay kāli mā kāli mā kāli mā

Victory to Mother Kali.

Amṛtapurēśvarī jaga jananī
amṛtapurēśvarī mama jananī

Goddess of Amritapuri, universal Mother, O my Mother.

Paramānanda samutthita madabhara
kalitamanōhara narttanalasitē
irukaikoṭṭi tālamurtirttatha
tērutērē naṭanam cēyvū mahēśi

Supreme Goddess, intoxicated with infinite bliss, You dance briskly and gracefully and clap Your hands.

Spandana śithilita kuntalajaṭilē
indukalōllasitōnnata niṭilē
jay jay kāli sanātana jananī
jay jay bhakta janāvana sujanī

Upon Your thick and long hair is a crown adorned with a crescent moon. Victory to Kali, the eternal Mother, the savior of devotees.

Jīvikal udayam cēyvatin mumbiha
dēvi kapālika mālayaṇiññōl
ulakinnuyirāy mēvinatāvaka
calanam pala pala jīvanidānam

O Goddess, adorned with a garland of human skulls, You have stood since the beginning of time. Your movements are the cause of creation.

JAY KALYĀṆĪ JAY BHAVĀNĪ (HINDI)

Jay kalyāṇī jay bhavānī
dēvi durgē mātā (2x)

Victory to the bestower of auspiciousness, victory to Goddess Bhavani. Victory to Divine Mother Durga.

Ambē mātā durgē mātā

O Mother, Mother Durga

Tum hō mā karuṇā kī mūrtti
dās kī sunalē vinati
samsara sē dē mā mukti
janma kā lakṣya kardē pūrtti

Mother, embodiment of compassion. Listen to the prayer of Your servant and liberate us from this samsara (cycle of births and deaths). Please fulfill the purpose of this human birth.

Dukhōn kī cintā dūr kardē
bhāva bhakti kā dilamē bhar dē
tava caraṇōmē karumē arpaṇ
tērēliyē mā hē yē jīvan

Please remove all worries and sorrows. Fill my heart with devotion towards You. I offer myself in worship at Your feet. Mother, this life is only for You.

JAY KALYĀṆĪ JAY BHAVĀNĪ (MARATHI)

Jay kalyāṇī jay bhavānī
dēvi durgē mātā (2x)

Victory to the bestower of auspiciousness, victory to Goddess Bhavani. Victory to Divine Mother Durga.

Ambē mātā durgē mātā

O Mother, Mother Durga

Mātē tu prēmācī mūrtti
udanḍa āyī tujhi kirti
samsārā tūn dēyī mukti
janmācē lakṣya hōyī pūrti

Mother, embodiment of love, listen to the prayer of Your servant and grant us liberation from this samsara (cycle of births and deaths). Please fulfill the purpose of this human birth.

Dukhāṅcī kālajī karu nakō rē
bhakticā bhāva tu sōḍū nakō rē
thakalēlyā manālā viśrānti dē rē
ambēcē smaraṇa karuna ghē rē

Please remove all worries and sorrows. Fill my heart with devotion towards You. I offer myself in worship at Your feet. Mother, this life is only for You.

Ayīcī kṛpā aśī nirālī
aṅdhār miṭēl yēyīl divāli
dār manācē ughaḍē asū dē
mātēlā tithē yēvūna basū dē

The grace of the Mother is infinitely great, it shall banish all darkness. The festival of lights will arise. Open the doors of the mind and enthrone the Divine Mother.

JINKI KARUṆĀ HĒ APĀR

Jinki karuṇā hē apār
jinki ānkhō mē hē pyār
jinkā darśan pā kē
sab hō jāyē nihāl
vō hē santōshi mā
mērī santōshi mā
jay santōshi mā

The Goddess whose compassion is infinite, whose eyes are full of love, whose darshan makes one's life blessed, She is Santoshi Ma. Salutations to You, O Mother.

Jinki mana mē hē viśvās
vahi mā mērī kartti hē vās
kōyi lōṭṭā nahīm udās
āyā mā jō tērē pās

sab samkata hāriṇi mā
jay santōshi mā

My Mother resides in the hearts of those who have faith. No one has returned sad on approaching the Mother. O, You who remove all obstacles, salutations to You, O Santoshi Ma.

Jō prēm sē śīś jukkāyē
mā unpar kṛpā tū barsāyē
yamdēv bhī unsē ghambarāyē
kabhī unhē vō chū nahī pāyē
śub kārini mā
jay santōshi mā

My Mother's grace flows to those who bow their heads in love at Her feet. Even the Lord of death is afraid to touch such devotees who have sought refuge with the Mother. You who bestow auspiciousness, salutations to You, Santoshi Ma.

Āvō mā kā nāma japē
bhāva sē unkī bhakti karē
sabmē mā kā rūpa dharē
dilsē unkī sēvā karē
bhavatāriṇi mā
jay santōshi mā

Come, let us chant the Mother's name. Let us sing Her glories with love. Let us serve humanity, beholding Her divine form in all beings. O, You who release us from the ocean of transmigration, salutations to You, O Santoshi Ma.

Prēm sē bōlō jay mātā kī
jhōr sē bōlō jay mātā kī
dil sē bōlō jay mātā kī
bhāv sē bōlō jay mātā kī

mil kē bōlō jay mātā kī
miṭhā bōlō jay mātā kī
sarē bōlō jay mātā kī
jay mātā kī jay mātā kī

Let us chant with love, victory to the Mother. Let us chant loudly ,victory to the Mother. Let us chant whole-heartedly, victory to the Mother. Let us chant with devotion, victory to the Mother. Let us chant in unison, victory to the Mother. Let us chant sweetly, victory to the Mother. Let us all chant together, victory to the Mother, victory to the Mother.

JĪVITAMENNUM

Jīvitamennum śōbhanamākkum
bhāvukadīpam nī ammē
jñāna tapasvikal tēṭumśāśvata
śāntinikētam nī

Mother, You are the lamp of love that always brightens life. You are the eternal abode of peace that the ascetics seek deep within themselves.

Prēma payasvini vēda manasvini
dēvi sarasvati nī ammē
phalavilōcini pāpavimārdhini
tāpavināśini nī

You are the river of love, O Devi Saraswati, You hold the Vedas in Your mind. You are the three-eyed Goddess who destroys sin and sorrow.

Nāda vinōdini vēda purātini
gāna vilōlini nī ammē
pāhiniranjjini yōga sugandhini
dēvi sanātani nī

You revel in music and song; You are as ancient as the Vedas. Protect us, O eternal Mother, You who are unblemished, who are filled with the fragrance of yoga.

Lōka kṛpānidhi jñāna kalānidhi
kāvya payōdadhi nī ammē
dīnadayāmayī dhyēyasudhāmayī
snēhadayāmayī nī

You are the abode of compassion for one and all, the treasurehouse of knowledge, arts and poetry. You are full of the sweet nectar of love and compassion and You are to be meditated upon.

Mānavajīvita nādavipañciyil
nūtanarāgam nī ammē
prēmarasāmṛta māripozhikkumo
rādimanādam nī

O Mother, You are the new melody emanating from the sonorous veena of human life. You are the primal sound that rains down as the nectar of love.

KAISĀ SANDĒŚĀ

Kaisā sandēśā tumdē gayē kānhā
mērē gōpiyōm kabhi āsūna bahānā
tujhē dēkhnē rādhā pyāsi jō rahatihē
āsuvōm kō pikē kūcha pyās bujhātihē

O Krishna, what kind of a message have You sent? "My dear Gopis, never shed tears." Radha is thirsty to see You and somehow quenches the thirst by drinking in the tears she sheds while remembering You.

Ēk pal jō bītē yug jaisā lagtāhē
tērē binā yē jīvan sūna lagtā hē
sāsōm kē chalnē kā nām hē jīnā tō
jī rahī hē rādhā samajh lēnā kṛṣṇā
kṛṣṇā kṛṣṇā

Even a single moment without You passes like a thousand years. This life is meaningless without You. If life is nothing more than simply breathing, then only on that condition can one say that Radha is alive. Understand this, O Krishna!

Tune jō kah diyā hastēhī rahnā
nahī hōtā mujhsē rōtē huyē hasnā
tērē sivā kōyi khuśi na jānu mē
tumhi hō sab kuch tērē caraṇōm ki dasi mē
kṛṣṇā kṛṣṇā

You have instructed us to keep smiling always. But it is difficult for me to laugh while crying. Radha doesn't know any other happiness than You. You are her all-in-all. Radha is the servant girl at Your feet.

KĀKKAI CIRAGINILĒ

Kākkai ciraginilē nandalālā - nintan
kariyaniram tōnṭrutayē nandalālā

Even in the blue-black feathers of the crow, O Nandalala, it is Your dark complexion I see.

Kēṭkkum oliyilellām nandalālā - nindan
gītam isaikkutaṭā nandalālā

In every sound that I hear, O Nandalala, it is Your song that I hear.

Pārkkum maraṅkalellām nandalālā
nandalālā (2x) - nintan
pachainiram tōnṭrutayē nandalālā

In every tree I observe, O Nandalala, it is Your emerald-green hue I see.

Tīkkul viralai vaittāl -
nandalālā - ninnai
tīṇṭuminpam tōnṭrutaṭa nandalālā

Even when I come near fire, O Nandalala, I feel that I am getting purified. As fire burns everything into ashes, You burn away all of my negativities.

Nandalālā hē nandalālā
vṛndāvana gōvinda bālā (2x)

O Nandalala, cowherd boy of Vrindavan.

KĀLAM KANALU

Kālam kanalu pozhikkunnu
jīvan taṇalu kotikkunnu
jīvita vīthiyil mullum pūvum
vāri vitaykkunnu vidhihitam
āru ninaykkunnu

Time (fate) brings pain like showers of fire. The soul yearns for the shelter of a shadow. The path of one's life is strewn with both flowers and thorns. Who knows what fate may have in store?

Ceytatinotta phalam nukarumbōl
ciri tūkum cilar karayum
niyati niyōgam karmmavipākam
nizhalukal pōl pintuṭarum

Some laugh and others weep while reaping the fruits of their actions. What fate decrees, what results our actions produce, follows us like a shadow.

Samamāy kāṇuka sukha dukhaṅgal
samaya vidhēyamitellām
anubhava mātrakal mārum nammal
anubhava sākṣikal mātram

Try to see happiness and sorrow as equal. All are subject to the will of time. Experiences last for a moment; we are only witnesses to our experiences.

Āśakal neyyum janimṛti pāśam
azhiyumbōl azhalozhiyum
ātmavicāra gatiyatha pulki
nukaruka paramānandam

Sorrow ends when we break the bondage of birth and death that is created through desires. Embrace the path of the contemplation of the Self and enjoy supreme bliss.

KĀLINDI KĀLIL

Kālindi kālil cilanpu keṭṭi
nīntumō bhūpālam mūli mūli
nīlakkadampukal pūṅkula kaikalāl
tūvumō vīṇṭumā tūmarandam

Will the Kalindi don anklets and swim, humming the bhupala raga once more? Will the blue kadamba flowers offer their sweet nectar once again?

Dūredūrettetō manassu tēṅgunnatin
dīnadīnasvanam nērttu kēlkkunnuvō

tāṇizhayunnilam tennalin lōlamām
tantriyilōlum orēkāntarōdanam

Far, far away, one can discern in the air the faint sobs of a sorrowing heart. The melancholy breeze, heavy with sorrow, bears with its sting a solitary wail.

Ātirappūkkal anāthamāyī
cūṭuvān rādha varāteyāyī
āśatan hṛnnīrkkuṭam takarnni malar
vāṭunnu saurabham cōrnnutīrnnu

The atira flowers wait forlornly for Radha, but she doesn't come anymore to wear them. All the hopes of Radha's heart have been shattered. O see this flower wilting, its fragrance run dry.

Rāgavilōla muraliyūti
rājīvanētran aṇaṅgiṭāykil
rādha varilla varāykilōrō mṛdu
tārum talirum talarnnuvīzhum

If the lotus-eyed one will not come, playing the soothing melodies of His flute, then Radha also will not come and each flower and bud will wilt and fall.

KAṆMALAR TIRANTU

Kaṇmalar tirantu kaṭaikaṇ pārttu
kavalaikal pōkka varūvāy kaṇṇā
manmakal kaṇavā malarmakal talaivā
malarpadam enakku taruvāy

O Kanna, come, open Your lotus eyes and remove all of my sorrows with the grace of Your glance. Lord of the Earth's daughter, Lord of Laksmi, grant that I may catch hold of Your blessed feet.

Kalla chakaṭanai kālāl utaitta
kallai ponnāy kanintiṭa ceydha
pulvāy pilantu bhūtalam kātti
pollā marattai sāytta kaṇṇā

O Kanna, You killed Sakatasura, You revealed the whole universe in Your own little mouth and You turned stone into pure gold.

Vānavar vāzhvu sirantiṭa ceyya
vānamud inta nandakumārā
dānavar serukkinai ozhitida vēṇṭi
dasāvatāram eṭutta amarā

O Nandakumara, You distributed the nectar of immortality to the Devas to uplift them, and You incarnated ten times to destroy the egos of the demons.

Āychiyar azhaikka ōṭiyē vantāy
anpōṭu unnai anaittiṭa varuvāy
kāychiya pālōṭu tayirum taruvēn
kaṇṇē maṇiyē vēdanai tīrppāy

You who responded to the call of the Gopis, please come before me also so that I can lovingly embrace You. O my darling precious one, I'll give You milk and curd. Please remove my sorrows.

KAṆṆAṆAI KANDĀYŌ NĪ

Kaṇṇaṇai kandāyō nī tōzhi
annayin ātankam nī ariyāy kaṇṇā
alli aṇaittiṭavē ēnkukinṭrāl

My dear friend, did you see Kanna? O Kanna, don't You know the yearning of Your mother? She is yearning to take You into her arms.

Yaśōdhai annai azhaikinṭrāl
anpu kaṇṇā nī enku cenṭrāy
paśukkalai mēykka nī cenṭrāyō
bālā līlaikkāy cenṭrāyō
avalai kaikalil vaittu koṇṭu
anpuṭan tēṭi alaikinṭrāl

Mother Yashoda is calling You, dearest Kanna, where did You go? Did You go with the cattle for grazing? Or did You go to play some childlike pranks? She is searching for You and holding flattened sweet rice in her hands to give to You.

Veṇṇai uṇṇa nī cenṭrāyō
vēṇugānattil marandāyō
pinnāl varukinṭra gōpiyarin
piriyattil avalai marandāyō
rādhāyai tēṭi cenṭrāyō anta
rāgattil tāyai marantāyō

Did You go to eat butter or did You lose Yourself in the music of Your flute? Did You forget Your mother due to the intense longing of the Gopis or is it because You have gone in search of Radha?

Yamunātīra vihāri jay
vṛndāvana sañcāri jay
gōvarddhana giridhāri jay
gōpālā kṛṣṇā murāri jay

Victory to Krishna, who plays on the banks of the Yamuna river and roams in the city of Vrindavan. Victory to the cowherd boy who lifted the Govardhana Mountain.

KAṆṆĀ VĀ VĀ VĀ

Kaṇṇā vā vā vā muki loli varṇṇā vā vā vā

Come, Kanna, come, You with the complexion of a dark rain cloud, come.

Tirumuṭiyil taru pilikal cūṭi
kēli kalāṭi vana murali kayil
rāgam tālam pallavi pāṭi
kaṇṇa vā vā vā muki loli
varṇṇā vā vā vā

A resplendent peacock feather adorns Your head and You play sweet music on Your enchanting flute. Come Kanna, come dark-complexioned one.

Kilu kile kiluṅguṇa kālttala nādam
madhuram nirayum puñciri rūki
arayil kiṅgiṇi cārttiyoruṇī
kaṇṇa vā vā vāmuki loli
varṇṇā vā vā vā

With the sound of Your ringing anklets, with a honey-filled smile on Your lips, wearing a beautiful belt around Your waist, come Kanna, come.

Tarivala kiṅgiṇi tālamuyarnnu
mañ peṭṭu ṭayāṭayaṇiṇa
mathi varuvōlam veṇṇa nukarnna
kaṇṇā vā vā vā muki loli
varṇṇā vā vā vā

O Krishna, dressed in yellow, You eat butter until You are fully satisfied. Come before us, Kanna, come dark-complexioned one.

KAṆṆĪR KAṬALUKAL

Kaṇṇīr kaṭalukal nīntikkaṭannu ñān
kannā nin tīramaṇaññu
enkilum en vidhi etra bhayānakam
agni mēghaṅgalen cuttum nāthā
nin virahāgni varṣippū

O Kanna, I have swum across oceans of tears to reach Your shore. Yet, alas, how frightening is my fate. O Lord, fiery clouds from all sides are feeding the fire of seperation.

Janmavalli kkuṭil tōrum naṭannu ñān
ninne tiraññu karaññu
enniṭṭum en munnil onnu vannīṭāte
eṅgō maraññu nilkkunnu kaṇṇā
entē maraññu nilkkunnu

I wandered, searching for You through the tangled vines of many births. Where are You hiding, O Kanna, without coming before me? Why are You still hiding?

En cuṭu vīrppukal ētu vāṅgīṭṭitā
chilli mulankāṭu tēṅgi
en kitappatrayum ētu vāṅgīṭṭitā
kālindiyum kitaykkunnu kaṇṇā
nin kṛpamātramillenno

See how the bamboo forest is lamenting to bear my hot perspiration and the river Kalindi is panting, having taken on my breathlessness. O Kanna, is it only Your grace that I lack?

KARA LŌ NAIYĀ PĀRA

Kara lō naiyā pāra hamāre
jaga kē pālaka mērē rām

Please take this boat of life across the ocean of Samsara to the eternal shores, O protector of the world, Lord Rama.

Śrī rām jay rām jay jay rām (4x)

O Lord Rama, salutations to You.

Jō gāyē prabhu tērī mahimā
māyā jāl sē mukti pāyē
jō ban jāyē dās tumhārō
sachā dhan bas vō hī pāyē

One who sings Your glories is liberated forever from the vicious trap of maya (delusion). One who becomes Your servant alone earns the true wealth in this world.

Kab hē mērī bārī rām
darśana dēnā mērē rām
basa jāō mērē mana mē rām
dēra na karanā sītārām

When is my turn to get Your darshan, O Rama. Please come and reside in my heart without any delay.

Jin ānkhō mē ram jāyē rām
rām kā darśan sab mē pāyē
dukha kā har kaṇa sab miṭa jāyē
brahmānanda hī bas raha jāyē

If one's eyes are filled with Lord Rama, he sees the Lord alone in everyone. Even the smallest trace of sorrow is removed; divine bliss alone remains.

Kab hē mērī bārī rām
darśan dēnā mērē rām
bas jāō mērē man mē rām
dēra na karanā sītārām

When is my turn to get Your darshan, O Rama. Please come and reside in my heart without any delay.

Sīta rām rām rām (4x)
bolo rām rām rām (4x)

Let us sing the Lord's name, Ram, Ram, Ram.

KARAYUM KĀRMUKIL

Karayum kārmukil kaṇṭāl mātram
pīli viṭarttum mayilē
āśāḍhamēghamāy ñān nilkkunnu
āṭū kṛṣṇā mayilē
ente dukhattil sānandamāṭū

O peacock, you spread your feathers only at the sight of weeping clouds. I stand here as a monsoon cloud. Dance as would Krishna, O peacock, remove my sorrow with bliss.

Nirayum kālindi tīrattāṭān
kotikku nīlamayilē
enśrudhārā kālindi tīratta
āṭū kṛṣṇā mayilē
ente dukhattil sānandamāṭū

O blue peacock, come dance on the shore of the Kalindi river, the Kalindi which is a stream of tears. Dance as would Krishna, O peacock, remove my sorrow with bliss.

Śōka nikuñjattil kaṇṇīr kanikal
tēṭiyiṅgettu mayilē
tṛptil kāruṇya kēkāravattil
āṭū kṛṣṇā mayilē
ente dukhattil sānandamāṭū

O peacock, you search for teardrops in the depths of my sorrow. Sing your song of mercy. Dance as would Krishna, O peacock, remove my sorrow with bliss.

Hē giridhāri kṛṣṇā murārī
viraha vṛndāvanacārī
ennārtta hṛttil vṛndāvaniyil
āṭū kṛṣṇā mayilē
ente dukhattil sānandamāṭū

O Krishna, who upheld the Giridhari Mountain and wandered through Vrindavan, come to the Vrindavan of my grieving heart. Dance as would Krishna, O peacock, remove my sorrow with bliss.

KARPPŪRADĪPAM

Karppūradīpam tozhutu nilkkumbōl
ullattileṅgō ñān mōhichu
ammē, dēvi, amṛtavarṣiṇi,
karppūram āyirunneṅkil, ñānā
karppūram āyirunneṅkil!

While standing in reverence before the burning camphor lamp, from somewhere deep inside of me arose a desire. Amme, Devi, Amritavarshini, if only I was that camphor, if only I was that camphor.

Sādhakanallivanammē, janma -
vēdanayenne grasippū.
nīrum manassinnorāśvāsam ēkuvān
tūmandahāsam pozhikkū, māyē,
tūmandahāsam pozhikkū

O Mother, this one is no sadhak; the pain of life overcomes him. To grant a little bit of solace to the sorrowful mind, shower Your graceful smile, O Mother of illusion, shower Your graceful smile.

Bhōgāśayērunnu nīle - pinne
tyāgāśayētumēyilla
kālam vṛthāvilāvunnu dayāmayī,
cārattaṇayāttatentē, dēvi,
cārattaṇayāttatentē?

The desire for enjoyment continues to rise up incessently, quenching the desire for renunciation. Time is thus exhausted in waste, O Compassionate One, why don't You come to me, Devi, why don't You come to me?

KARUṆĀMAYĪ SNĒHA ARUṆŌDAYAM

Karuṇāmayī snēha aruṇōdayam ñān
śaranāgati ninte charaṇālayē
amṛtēśvarī annapūrṇṇēśvarī enṭe
hṛdayam nī, ñān cheyta pūjāphalam

O compassionate Mother, You are the awakener of love. I surrender at Your sacred feet. Immortal Goddess, Goddess of nourishment, please grant me the bliss of worshipping You within my heart.

Śāradāmbikē śravanē madhurāmayī
śivasundarī śōka rōga vināśinī
sādhūjana paripālakē ātmīyabhōdha
prakāśa prasāda prasīda mē

Mother Sarada, Mother of the Vedas, sweet, beautiful and auspicious one, You destroy all sorrows and diseases. Benefactor of the virtuous, O effulgent and supreme consciousness, be pleased with me.

Añcātē nin śakti arivanāy cilaraṅgu
pañcāmṛtattināy kāttuninnīṭavē
añcuviral kāṭṭi nī abhayakaram nīṭṭi nī
cāñcāṭum verum pātram akṣayapātramākki nī

To experience Your divine energy, some eat the prasad made of five sugars. With five fingers, You show the sign of protection from fear. An empty vessel in Your hands becomes everlasting and ever-full.

Vēdyāsakula jātayām nin tiru
vaibhavam kāṇānāy nin kulavāsikal
vēdanayōṭaṅga matsyam cōdikkavē
vembum kaṭal matsyamaṇḍalam ākki nī

You were born in the clan of sage Veda Vyasa. When the poor fishermen of Your village asked for food, You changed the violent ocean into a world abounding in fish.

KĀRUṆYA PĪYŪṢADHĀMAM

Kāruṇya pīyūṣadhāmam, amma
kāṇappeṭunnātma tatvam
ñānenna bhāvam naśichātmasamśuddhi
nēṭunnavar kāṇmu satyam

Mother, the abode of nectarous compassion, is the truth of our inner self manifested before us. Those who obliterate the ego sense and attain the state of mental purity, come to perceive this truth.

Kāṭṭunnu nērāya mārgam, amma -
yēkunnu nityāvabōdham
mārum prapañcattinādhāramāy mēvum -
ānandamūrtē tozhunnēn

Mother shows us the right path and bestows upon us eternal knowledge. O embodiment of bliss, substratum of this changing universe, I salute Thee.

Tīrtthaṅgalil kulikkēṇṭa, ghōra -
ghōram tapam ceytiṭēṇṭa,
ammayil mānasam cemmēyurappichu
dhanyamāy tīrkkuvin janmam!

Neither is it necessary to immerse oneself in the holy waters nor undergo severe austerities; to make one's life blessed, keep the mind firmly centered upon Mother!

KAṬALŌRAM TAPAMCEYYUM

Kaṭalōram tapamceyyum kāliyammā
kanivōṭu emai kākkum śaktiyammā
maṭal virikkum tāzhai ena bhaktivellam
maṇpathayil pāychukintra śaktiyammā

O Mother Kali, You engage in severe penance on the shore of the ocean. You are the supreme energy that lovingly protects all of us. You are flooding the whole Earth with the river of divine love.

Piraviyenum kaṭal kaṭakka tōṇi āvāi
pirpaṭṭōr nalam peravē ēṇi āvāi
marati enum mayakkathai pōkkiṭuvāi
manathil irai cintanaiyai valarttiṭuvāi

You are the boat on which we can cross the ocean of birth and death. You are a ladder for ignorant people to use to reach the goal. Filling our minds with thoughts of God, You awaken us from our slumber of forgetfulness.

Uravu solli tiruvaṭiyai pattrinirppōr
uyarvaṭaya varam taruvāl entrum aval
turaviyarum pōṭṭrukintra tūyavalē
teviṭṭāta pērinbam tarupavalē

For one who depends solely on You, You give the boon of prosperity forever. You are praised even by great ascetics. You give eternal bliss to everyone.

KITĪ ĀNANDA RĒ

Kitī ānanda rē paramānanda rē
tujhē nāmāchē guṇagān
jay rām jay rām jay śrīrām
raghupati rāghava rājā rām

O Rama, glory to You, what a supreme bliss it is to sing Your divine name.

Jay jay rām rām rām sita rām
jay jay rām rām rām sita rām

Victory to Lord Rama.

Dōn akṣarānchē nām tujhē
mahimā tyācī śabdāmcyā pār

pāpāmcē bhār jāvē miṭūn
jō mhaṇē jay śrī rām

Your blessed name has just two syllables but Your greatness is beyond words. The burden of sins is removed for those who chant the name "Ram."

Manāta jyācē gumjatē rām
tithē prabhucē mangala dhām
manāta jyācē dāsālā bhāv
tithē viśrām kartō ram

The glorious Lord resides in one whose inner realm resonates with the word "Ram." The Lord rests in the heart of one who is humbler than the humblest.

Japu sadā mī nām tujhē
ruci tyāci vāḍhavū dē rām
divya rūpācē darśan dē ūn
tujhyāśī ēka karun gē rām

May I chant Your name always, Lord Ram, let the desire to chant grow stronger in me. By granting me the glorious vision of Your form, please make me one with You.

KṚṢṆĀ MURĀRI (YAMUNĀ TĪRA)

Kṛṣṇā murāri vrindāvana sañcāri
vrindāvana sañcāri

O Krishna, who destroyed the demon, Mura; in the city of Vrindavan You wander freely.

Yamunā tīra vihāri
vṛndāvana sañcāri
gōvarddhanōddari
gōpālā kṛṣṇā murāri

Krishna, who travels along the course of the Yamuna river and roams through the city of Vrindavan, You upheld the great mountain Govardhana, O cowherd boy, You killed the evil demon, Mura.

Ippirappu pōnāl enakku
eppīrappu vāykkumō kaṇṇā
oppuyarvillata ōmkāra
kuzhalisaippāyappā kaṇṇā

If I miss my chance in this present birth, then when will I ever again have the opportunity to hear the incomparable sound of the "Omkar" that emanates from Your flute when You play upon it.

Tappāmal uyirinaṅkallellām tanai marantu
irukkum appōdu nān ciru pullāy - kallāki
pullākavō anri kallākavō irukka vēṇṭum

In that moment all will forget themselves. I should at least be present, even if I be nothing more than a grass or a stone.

Azhakiya vṛndāvanam taniloru
pullāy piravi tara vēṇṭum
kaṇṇā punitamāna pala kodi piravi tandālum
vṛndāvana matiloru pullāy piravi tara vēṇṭum

O grant that I may be born in the blessed city of Vrindavan as nothing more than a mere patch of grass! You may give hundreds of thousands of births to me, but grant that I am born as the grass in Vrindavan.

Pullāyinum nedunāl nillātu - enavē
kallāy piravi tara veṇṭum - oru cira
kallāy piravi tara vēṇṭum

But if it be grass, then that birth will surely pass quickly. Thus, let me be born as a stone!

Kamala malariṇaikal anaya enatu ullam pulakitamutriḍum bayamatriṭum ena oru pullay

When I behold Your divine form, adorned with lotus flowers, my heart is thrilled and I become fearless. O Krishna, grant that I may take birth as nothing more than the grass or a stone in Vrindavan.

KṚṢṆANAI BHAJANAI ŚEYVĀY

Kṛṣṇanai bhajanai śeyvāy manamē dinamē
kṛṣṇanai bhajanai śeyvāy

O mind, worship Krishna! Worship Krishna every day.

Vṛṣṇi vamśaja vraja samrakṣaka
rādhā ramaṇanai bhajanai śevāy

Born among the Vrishnis, He is the saviour of the cowherds and the beloved of Radha. O mind, worship Krishna.

Gōpi vallabha gōkūla pālanai
gōpari pālanai bhajanai śevāy

The friend of the Gopis, the refuge of Gokul and of the cows, O my mind, worship Him.

Kāliya marddanai kamśa vidhvamsanai
dvāraka pālanai bhajanai śevāy

By dancing on the raised hood of the serpent Kaliya, He destroyed its ego. O mind, worship Him who vanquished Kamsa, worship the saviour of Dwaraka.

Pāṇḍava rakṣaka kauravaśikṣaka
pūrandara viṭhalanai bhajanai śevāy

By Him were the righteous Pandavas saved and the treacherous Kauravas destroyed. O mind, worship Him who stands in the Pandarpur temple as Purandhara Vithalla.

KUCHA NA LĒ

Kuch na lē āyā tū
kuch na lē jāyēgā
nām hari kā japa lē
samga vahī āyēgā

O man, when you came into this world you had nothing. You will leave this Earth in the same condition. Thus, chant the name of Lord Hari. Only He will accompany us.

Hari bōl hari bōl hari hari bōl (2x)

Chant the name of Hari

Hōgā kyā kal yē
na tujhakō khabar hai
kuch dinōm ka hai rē
jīvan safar yē

You do not know what tomorrow will bring. This life itself is merely a journey of a few days.

Samay na gavā
ab tō hari hari bōl (2x)

Do not waste anymore time, start chanting the name of Hari.

Sukha mē sab sāth rahē
dukha mē na kōyī rē
apanē sē badkar
na prēm karē kōyī rē

In good times, there will be many well wishers in your life. But when bad times come there will be nobody to offer you any support. Nobody loves another more than oneself.

LĒ LŌ ŚARAṆA MĒ MĀ

Lē lō śaraṇa mē mā
jananī hē jagadīśvarī mā
tum hō saba kuch mā mērī
mātā pitā guru īśvara bhī

O Mother, grant me refuge, O Goddess of the universe. You mean everything to me. You are my Mother, Father, Guru and God.

Dūr karō mā jaga kī māyā
ab tō mujhkō dē dō sahārā
tava caraṇō mē śaraṇāgat kō
thōdī jagah tō dēnā maiyā

Remove, O Mother, the delusion of this cycle of birth and death. Please give me the support to rise. O Mother, won't You bless this refugee by granting him a little place at Your lotus feet !

Jay jagadambē mangala dāyinī
abhaya pradāyinī mērī mā

Salutations to the Divine Mother, the bestower of auspiciousness, the bestower of eternal refuge.

Rōtā śiśu jab mā kō pukārē
chōḍ kē saba kucha mā dauḍh āyē
sārē jaga kī tuma hō mātā
kyō hē dērī darśan dē dō

When a little crying child calls for his Mother, the Mother, leaving everything, comes running towards him. O Mother, You are the Mother of the whole universe. Why delay in granting Your vision?

MAHĀDĒVĀ ŚAMBHŌ MAHĒŚĀ

Mahādēvā śambhō mahēśā manōjñā
mṛḍā manmathārē mahākālamūrttē
śivā śamkarā śarva sarvātmarūpā
samastēśvarā śūlapāṇē namastē

O Great God, Siva, beautiful God, the slayer of Kamadeva, the great Lord of destruction, auspicious one, residing in all beings. Prostrations to the Lord of all who holds His trident in his hands.

Umākānta kailāsa vāsākṛpālō
kapālī kalādhāri kāruṇyasindhō
bhavā bhasmabhūṣāmga bhaktāntaramgā
bhujamgapriyā bhūtanāthā namastē

Lord of Uma, residing on Mount Kailas, the ever compassionate one, holding a skull bowl, wearing the crescent moon, overflowing with compassion, of exalted moods, with sacred ash smeared all over Your body, the inner Self of the devotees. Salutations to the Lord of Spirits, who is fond of snakes.

Jaḍābhūṣitā janavītīravāsā
jagannāyakā brahma jīvasvarūpā
guṇātīta gamgādharā gauravarṇṇā
gaṇādhīśa gaurīpriyā tē namastē

Whose hair is in knots, who resides on the shore of the Ganga river, the Lord of the world, the essence of the individual Self and the supreme Self, who is beyond all qualities. The white-skinned one who carries the Ganges on his head. Prostrations to the husband of Gauri, the Lord of ghosts and spirits.

Paśunāmpatē pāpanāśā pavitrā
prapañcēśvarā pārvatī prāṇa nāthā
prabhō patmanābhārchitā bhāvagamyā
bhavānīsamētā namaste namastē

Lord of all beings, destroyer of sins, eternally pure one, Lord of creation, life of Parvati, the Lord of devotion who is worshipped by Vishnu, salutations to the companion of Bhavani.

MĀHIṢĀSURA MARDINI

Māhiṣāsura mardini
mahapātaka nāśini
praṇatarti vināśini
pranavābdhi vihāriṇi

You who destroyed the demon Mahisha, You who incinerate even enormous sins, the destroyer of the grief of those who prostrate, You who reside in the sacred ocean of the Pranava mantra, O Devi.

Malayācala vāsini
mamatā madanāśini
satcinmaya rūpiṇi
śaranāgata pālini

You who reside in the mountainous regions, who destroy the disease of ego, the embodiment of pure consciousness, You protect those who surrender to You.

Pāhimām jagadīśvarī
dehimē karunāmṛtam

Protect me, O Goddess of the universe. Grant me the nectar of Your compassion.

Jñānāmṛtadāyini
janidukha vināṣini
karuṇāmṛta varṣini
kāli kanmaṣa nāṣini

You who dispense the ambrosia of eternal knowledge, who destroy the misery of repeated births and deaths and shower the bliss of unconditional compassion, You destroy the sorrow of this Kali Yuga.

Vēdāmṛta rūpiṇi
varadē abhayamkari
caraṇāmbujam ambā tē
śaraṇam mama santatam

O embodiment of the bliss of the Vedas, You who bestow boons and grant protection, Your sacred feet are my sole refuge for all of eternity.

Santatam vandanam jagadambikē

I offer my salutations to the Mother of the universe.

MAHITA SNĒHAM

Mahita snēham pakarnnun ammē
punitamākkunnu amma
duritapūrṇṇa hṛdaya bhāram

pakaramēlkkunnu

Mother blesses us with Her divine love and lifts the sufferings and burdens from our hearts.

Iṭari vīzhātiṭavazhiyil
karamaṇaykkunnu amma
arikiluṇṭannarumavākyam
bhayam akatunnu

Mother extends Her hands and guards us from faltering and falling down on our path. She removes our fears with Her loving words.

Mativitumbi mizhitulumbi
ciriyoṭuṅgumbōl amma
arikiletti mizhituṭacha
gatitelikkunnu

When our hearts ache, our eyes brim with tears and our laughter fades, Mother comes to our side, wipes our tears and shows us the way.

Kanaleriyum karalilamma
karuṇatūkunnu ārum
aruma makkal bhuvanam
ammaykkoru kutumbam tān

Mother sprinkles Her soothing mercy on the burning embers in our hearts. All are Her darling children; all belong to Her one universal family.

Ila manassin telimayōṭā
padamalar tēṭum nammil
kanivoṭamma anubhavattēn
niravukākkunnu

With a full heart, let us search for those lotus feet. Mother guards the treasure of spiritual experience within us.

Smaraṇatan pūntaṇalu māyātoru
varam nalkū ammē
karalilennum teliyumaṅgē
mahima pāṭaṭṭe

Let us seek the boon that the golden remembrance of Mother may stay constant within us. O Mother, we celebrate Your greatness with constant songs in our hearts.

MĀ JAGADAMBĒ

Mā jagadambē darśan tērē
dhanya bhāg mērē
kṛpā jō tērī rahē sadā tō
tar jāyē andhērē

O Mother of the universe, I would be blessed and fortunate indeed to secure Your divine vision. If Your divine grace flows towards me always I shall swim across the darkness.

Mujhē prēm dō jagadambē
bhakti dō jagadambē
viśvās dēkar mērī
rakṣā karō jagadambē

O Divine Mother, give me pure love. O Divine Mother, give me devotion. O Divine Mother, protect me by giving me perfect faith.

Tērī ēk jhalak sē mayā
pulkit huvē sabhī
tērē binā mē ēk pal bhī
jīnā saku kabi

Just a single glimpse of You, O Mother, thrills me to the core. Without You, O Mother, I cannot live for a single instant.

Yē jīvan hē vyarth mērā
tērā sāth binā
man mē hē ēkhi ās
tujhsē hē milna

Without Your divine company, this life of mine is but a waste. All that I long for in my heart is to merge with You.

Tū jīvan kā sār mērā
tū hī mērā pyār
caraṇō mē tērē sadā rahūn
karnā yē upkār

You are the essence of my life. You are my true love. Please favour me by keeping me forever at Your holy feet.

MĀ JAY JAGADAMBĒ MĀ

Mā jay jagadambē mā jay
mā jay jagadambē mā
hē mātā bhavānī dēvi durgē
tērī jay jay kār

O triumphant Mother, Mother of the universe, victory to You. Salutations to Mother Bhavani, to Goddess Durga.

Mā tu mamatā ki mūrthi
mērī jīvan ki tu purthi
mā tu hē mērā darpan
mērā jīvan tērā arpan
tērē carnō kē dhul mē pakār
hō javum uddhār

O embodiment of love, You are the fulfillment of my life, I surrender myself to You. May my life be uplifted by touching the dust of Your revered feet.

Sānjha savērē tujhē pukaru mā
jai jagadambē mā
tērē caraṇōmē śiś jhukāvu
jai jagadambē mā
mujhē pās bulālē mā
mujhē apnā banā dē mā
mujhē apna banākē
is jīvan kō dhanya banādē mā

From dawn to dusk I chant Your name, O universal Mother, I prostrate before Your holy feet. Please make this life blessed by calling me close to You and making me Your own.

MĀ JAY MĀ KARLĒ JAPAN

Mā jay mā karlē japan
arpit karkē tu tan man
chōḍ dē jag kī tū lagan
mākō basā lē apanē man

Chant, 'Victory to Mother!' Surrender your body and mind to Her. Let go of your attachment to this world. Install Mother in your mind.

Māyā nē jō ghōrā man
rahā nahi mā kā sumiran
bīt rah hē har ēk kṣaṇ
vyarth na hō tērā jīvan

Due to delusion's sway over the mind you no longer remember Mother. But each moment is inexorably going by, don't let your life go to waste!

Jab tak hē mē ōr mērā
man mē hē bas andhērā

kahnā mā sab hē tērā
hō jāyēgā ujiyārā

As long as the feeling of 'I' and 'mine' exists, the mind will be full of darkness. Make the affirmation, 'O Mother, everything is Yours alone,' and, Lo! the light will flow into you.

Prēm sē bhaj lē mā nām
karnā dil sē tu praṇām
pāyēgā tu mā kā dhām
param śānti kā mangal dhām

Sing Mother's name with love, bow to Her from your innermost heart. Then you will reach Mother's abode, the auspicious haven of the highest peace.

MĀ KĪ NĀV

Mā kī nāv mē āvō bhaiyā
tārōm kē pār jāyēn
āvō, mākī gōd mē jāyēn

Come, my brother, let us climb into Mother's boat. We shall journey beyond the stars. Come, let us go to Mother's lap.

Ātmā kī yē yātrā
mā kī gōd mē pūrṇṇa hōyē
mā, jay mā, jay jay mā
mērī pyārī mā, ātma svarūpiṇi mā
mukti pradāyini mā
jay jagadīśvarī ma, jay jagadambē mā

The journey of the soul is fulfilled in Mother's lap. Victory to Mother! O beloved Mother, You are the embodiment of the Self, the bestower of liberation! Victory to the Queen of the universe! Victory to the Mother of the universe.

Prēm svarūpiṇi mā kē jaisē
jag mē aisa kōyī nahī rē
mā, jay mā, jay jay mā mērī
pyārī mā, hṛdaya nivāsini mā
bhakti pradāyini mā
jay jagadīśvarī ma, jay jagadambē mā

Mother is the personification of love; there is no one in the world like Her. Victory to Mother! O beloved Mother, You dwell in the heart, You grant devotion! Victory to the Queen of the universe! Victory to the Mother of the universe!

MANGALA VARADĀ

Mangala varadā gajānanā
samkata haraṇā śubhānanā
pārvati tanayā gajānanā
pāpa vimōcanam tava nāmam

You who bestow auspiciousness, O Ganesha, endowed with the face of an elephant, You destroy all sorrows, O auspicious one. Son of Parvati, Your name saves us from all sins.

Mōdaka rasikā gajānanā
mōkṣa pradāyaka gajānanā
mōhana gātrā gajānanā
śōbhana caritā gajānanā

Modaka (a sweet preparation made of coconut, rice, sugar and ghee) is very dear to You. O Ganesha, You grant final liberation to Your supplicants. You shine radiantly and Your tale is glorious.

Śānta svarūpā sukha sadanā
sānanta naṭanā sat caraṇā

siddhi vināyaka śrī caraṇā
śiddhir dadhātu dayānidhē

O embodiment of peace, abode of happiness, blissful dancer, Your blessed feet are the symbols of truth. O Vinayaka, wielding subtle powers, grant us perfection. You are the eternally compassionate one.

MANAMIRUṆṬUVEN

Manamiruṇṭuven mānasamennapōl
varṣippū kaṇkalum mēghaṅgalum
pārine māri taṇuppikke kaṇṇunīr
mānasē tāpam valarttiṭunnu

The sky has become dark like my brooding mind. Both the clouds and my eyes are raining. Though the Earth is cooled by the soft rain, these tears only increase the heat that is burning my mind.

Entāṇu śyāmē varāttatennantikē
entinī kāṭhinya bhāvam ammē
sadyaḥ prasādinī nīyennu kēṭṭata
satyamallennu varikayāṇō

Why do You hesitate to come before me, O dark-complexioned one? Why do You show me such a hard heart? I have heard that You are easily pleased, but now it seems as if that is becoming untrue.

Artthikkunnilla aśassum kavitvavum
artthavum bhōga sukhaṅgalonnum
ammaye kāṇuvān arbhakanāśichāl
ammēyateṅgine kuttamākum

I don't ask for any fame or for the ability to write prose. I don't seek wealth or any of the sense pleasures. If the baby longs to see its Mother, is that a crime?

MANASĀ CĒYI SMARAṆA

Manasā cēyi smaraṇa ammanu
hē mana cēyi smaraṇa ammā
smaraṇa cēyi manasā

O mind, remember Mother.

Dēhaśuddhatā vākśuddhatā
manaḥ śuddhattā kāvālamṭē

If you want purity of body, speech and heart, O mind, remember Mother!

Rāgadvēṣamu kāmakrōdhamu
sukhadukhamu dāṭālamṭē

If you want to cross over attachment, hatred, joy and sorrow, O mind, remember Mother.

Manaḥśāntiyu samadṛṣṭiyu
buddhiśuddhiyu kāvālamṭē

If you want inner peace, equal vision and a pure intellect, O mind, remember Mother!

MANASSORU MĀYĀ

Manassoru māyā marīcika
atirezhātta marīcika
ariyātirikke nizhalpōltuṭarum
ariyumbōl verum marīcika
manassoru māyā marīcika

The mind is an illusionary, limitless mirage. When we are unaware of the mind, it follows us like a shadow. When we are aware of it, it is merely a mirage.

Vṛthayuṇarttīṭum sukhamuṇarttīṭum
āyiram anubhavatika yuṇarttīṭum
viṣayamallēlum viṣayiyumallanām
ariyumbōl varu marīcika
manassoru māyā marīcika

The mind causes sorrow, joy and thousands of experiences. We are not the objects of sensory experience, nor are we the ones who experience. The mind is merely a mirage.

Bhōga rasaṅgalil vīṇu naśikkum
tyāgatapagniyil nīri jvalikum
bandha vidhāyakam mōkṣasahāyam
ariyumbōl varu marīcika
manassoru māyā marīcika

The mind revels while immersed in the worldly pleasures. It burns in the fire of renunciation. It is the cause of bondage yet also the straight path to freedom. Our mind is merely an illusory mirage.

MĀṆIKKAKIṄKIṆI ĀRTHIA

Māṇikkakiṅkiṇi ārthia
āṇippon ārangal āṭiṭa
māṇiyām unnayē māvali
nāṇiyē enṭrumē pōṭrita

Even the fierce demon king Mahabali, ashamed of his own limited power in comparison to Your infinite glory, worships You. O Lord, Your beautiful anklets and the shaking of the golden necklaces and chains that adorn You make loud and sweet sounds.

Vārāy kaṇṇā vārāy
tārāy muttam tārāy

Come, Kanna, come, give a kiss.

Pañcavar dūtanāy śenṭravanē
nañcuṭai nākathai konṭravanē
pañcayar tuyaram tuṭaittavanē
añciṭum avalam tīrttavanē

O Krishna, the ambassador of the five Pandavas, You killed the poisonous snake, Kaliya. You removed the intense sorrows that plagued the Pandavas and You destroyed all of their fearful difficulties.

Āyarkulattinil tōnṭrivantāy
tāyar makhizhntiṭa āṭininṭrāy
vēyin kuzhalaye ūtivantāy
māyan isayinai pāṭivantāy

Born in a cowherd family, You made Your mother happy with Your dancing. O the player of the flute, king of Maya, You came playing the flute.

Ūnmaṇivāyināl pāṭīṭu nī
enmaṇivaṇṇane āṭiṭu nī
panmaṇi muttukal tantiṭu nī
en manakkōvilil taṅkiṭu nī

Sing with Your beautiful mouth, O my Manivarnna, dance. Grant me prosperity and reside in the innermost temple of my mind.

MĀNILĀTTĀYE

Mānilāttāye mādava
celvi tālē tālēlō
manpadhai kākkum
ādiyām śakti tālē tālēlō

O Mother, Mother of the Earth, the wealth of Vishnu, You are the saviour of mankind, O primordial power.

Pāṭiṭum pāṭṭil sērntiṭum
cuvayē tālē tālēlō
paramanin tuṇaiyē bhaktarin
uyirē tālē tālēlō

You are the sweetness of the songs which find utterance, O wife of Siva, You are the life of the devotees.

Vēlavan tāyāy mēdini
vantāy tālē tālēlō
śūlamē ēnti sukhattinai
tantāy tālē tālēlō

Mother of Lord Muruka, You have come to the world. Using Your trident, You removed all of the troubles and gave happiness to the world.

Madhurayai ālum mīnākṣi
nīyē tālē tālēlō
marattinai pōkkum jñānākṣi
tāyē tālē tālēlō

You are the Goddess Meenakshi of the city of Madurai. Endowed with the eye of wisdom, You remove the ignorance from us.

Dēviyāy vantu pāvaṅgal
nīkkum mātā tālēlō
tēṭiṭum ullam nāṭiṭa
ceyvāy dēvi tālēlō

Coming to us as the Goddess, You remove all of our sins. For minds that seek for the inner Truth, You come as the true source of happiness.

Pārvayāl ennai kātriṭum
amṛtē tālē tālēlō
pārinil vanta ānanda
mayamē tālē tālēlō

You save me with Your glance, O immortal one, embodiment of bliss, descend on Earth.

MAṆIVARṆṆAN VANNĪLA

Maṇivarṇṇan vannīla varadānam tannīla
manatāril vanamāli madhumāri peytīla
mānasam śilayākki rādhaye tanichākki
rāgavilōlan ineṅgu pōyi ente
jīvita vēṇurāgam eṅgu pōyi

O my emerald Krishna has not come, He has not showered His boons on me. Vanamali has not showered nectar in my heart. Is His heart of stone that He has left Radha to pine all alone? Where has He gone, the flute player, He who is the melody of my soul, where has He gone?

Śrī kṛṣṇā jay kṛṣṇā gōvinda murārē (2x)
kṛṣṇā gōvinda

Victory to Krishna, the tender of the cows and the slayer of demons.

Vanavallikal pūtta varṇṇamayūkhaṅgal
yamunayilōlattil tulumbinilkkē
ñān ariyāte ente pūmaṇivīṇa tānē
pāṭunna bhāva gītam ārakku vēṇṭi

As the play of the colours of freshly blossomed wild flowers dance merrily in the waves of the Yamuna River, the veena of my heart spontaneously plays its sad and soulful tune, but for whom?

Kalavēṇu madhugāna svaramāriyil mōha
mayilvṛndam mayilppīli kuṭanivartti
ilam tennalūyalāṭum karayile kadambaṅgal
ōrmmayilennumennil malar virichu

In the rainfall of the flute's sweet melodies, my heart danced like a peacock with its feathers drawn. The kadamba flowers, nodding in the gentle breeze, awaken in me a thousand memories of Krishna.

MAṆṆŌRKKUM VIṆṆŌRKKUM

Maṇṇōrkkum viṇṇōrkkum
kaṇṇāna kaṇṇanē
mankāta vilakkāy en
akattē vilankiṭu

O Kanna, who is like the eye of the earthly and heavenly beings, please shine in my heart always like a light that never becomes dim.

Uzhvinayai aruthiṭavē
maṇṇil vanta amutamē
turavu chuṭar vilakkamāka
vāzhntu kāṭṭum kumudamē

O embodiment of ambrosia, You have come to sever the chain of evil destiny. O Lotus-like God, You live on as the radiant light of renunciation.

Kuzhalūti gōkulathin ā
kulathai īrtha kannā
ākulathai tīrthu entan
vāzhvai punitamākkuvāy

O Kanna, You enchanted even the cows in Gokula by playing your divine flute. Please remove my sorrows and make my life blessed.

Arakkarin kulam azhithu
aram valartta mannanē
arivu petru tāṭkal cērum
nāṭkal eṇṇi vāzhukirēn

O King, who destroyed the race of demons and nourished the eternal Dharma, I live counting the days until I will gain the imperishable knowledge and merge in Your holy feet.

Gōpālā bālā gōpījana lōla
vṛndāvana bālā bhakta paripālā

O cowherd boy, the playmate of the Gopis. O child of Vrindavan, You are the protector of the devotees.

MĀYAIYENṬRA PĒYINAI

Māyaiyenṭra pēyinai ōṭṭiṭavum nam
manatil inbam cērttiṭavum
mangala dēvataiyāka vantāl nam
maṭamaiyai ellām pōkkavantāl

Our Mother has come as the Goddess of auspiciousness to chase away the ghost of illusion and to fill us with happiness. She has come to destroy our ignorance.

**Ammā ammā enṭrazhaikkayile
akamum kulirndu pōkutammā
amṛtamozhikalai kēṭkayile
anaittum marantu pōkutammā**

When I call out, "Mother, Mother," my mind experiences a soothing coolness. When I hear Mother's immortal words, I forget everything else in the world.

**Idayamām kōvilil kuṭiyēttrī
inbamāy gītam pāṭiṭuvōm
bandhamkal pōkkiṭum tāyavalin
pādam paṇindu vāzhthiṭuvōm**

Let us consecrate Mother in the temple of our heart and sing happily. Let us surrender and glorify the Mother who cuts away all bondage.

MĒRĪ DHAḌKAN TĒRĀ NĀM

**Mērī dhaḍkan tērā nām
inmē antar kyā hē rām
sānsō kī yē dhārā tērī
har sāns bōlē jay śrī rām**

O Ram, my heart beat and Your hallowed name have become synchronised with one another. The flow of each and every breath of mine comes from You. Each breath chants "Praise Lord Ram".

**Jay śrī rām jay śrī rām
jay jay jay jay jay śrī rām**

Praise Lord Ram, Praise Lord Ram

Man kē antaranga mē
tū hi muskurāyē rām
tērē divya prakāś sē
khil uṭhā hē man kā dhām

O Lord Ram, in the innermost temple of my mind You alone smile. In the radiance of Your divine presence my mind has fully blossomed.

Pūrā viśva manca hē
tērī līlā kā hē rām
tērē pāvan hāthō sē
hō rahē hēsārē kām

O Ram, the entire universe is but a stage for Your divine play. All the actions are being performed by Your pure hands.

MŌRĒ LĀGĒ

Mōrē lāgē naṭaka guru caraṇa na kī
caraṇa binā mujhē kachu nahi bhāvē
jhūṭha māyā saba sapanan kī

My heart overflows with love for the lotus feet of the Guru. I don't know anything other than the Guru's feet. The illusion of this world, it is all merely a dream.

Ōm guru mātā sat guru mātā amṛtānandamayī
jay guru mātā śrī guru mātā amṛtānandamayī

Victory Mata Amritanandamayi, the exalted and supreme Guru.

Bhava sāgara saba sūka gayā hai
phikara nahi mujhē taraṇa na kī

The ocean of transmigration has dried up, thus I need no longer fear crossing it.

Mīrā kahē prabhu giridhāra nāgara
ulaṭa bhauyē mōrē nayana kī

O Lord, You who have lifted the Govardhana mountain, Meera has assumed the pose of a divine mood.

MUJHKŌ KṢMĀ

Mujhkō kṣmā karō (2x)
mērē aparādhōm kō kṣmā karō

O Mother, please forgive me! Kindly forgive all my errors.

Śaraṇa śaraṇa tērī caraṇa hī mā tērī
caraṇa rahē mērē man mē sadā
mālum nahī mujhē kaisē arpit hōnā
samjhāvō mērī mā tērī nalhī bachī kō

I seek refuge at Your feet, my only sanctuary. May Your sacred feet remain in my mind always. I do not know how to surrender. O my Mother; please show this tiny child the way.

Dayā karō kṛpā karō
rakṣā karō mērī karō

O Mother, grant me Your grace and protect me.

MURALĪ DHARA SUNDARA

Muralī dhara sundara rūpam
hari candana carcita gātram
yamunātaṭa kuñjavihāram
yadunāthā manam gasamāmgam

O Lord of beautiful form, with the flute clasped in Your hands, Your body is soft and anointed with sandal paste. Dwelling along the shores of the river Yamuna, the Lord of the Yadus, Your body is similar in form to that of Cupid's.

Śaraṇāgatavatsala hṛdayam
mṛduhāsa manōhara vadanam
karuṇā rasa pūrit nayanam
vanasūna vibhūṣita cikuram

Your heart is overflowing with affection; in You do the devotees take refuge. A soft, auspicious smile illumines Your face and Your eyes are full of compassion. Newly bloomed wildflowers adorn Your hair.

Kamalāpari lālita caraṇam
gajarājavirajita gamanam
vrajagōpavadhū priya ramaṇam
raṇanirjita dānavanikaram

The Goddess Lakshmi massages Your tender feet. When walking, You appear like a mighty elephant. You are the dearest companion of the Gopis who reside in Vrindavan. In battle, You have destroyed all demons.

Śaraṇāgatapālana niratam
bhavasāgara tāraṇanipuṇam
paśupālaka bālakam aniśam
hṛdi bhāvaya bhāvaka varadam

You are the eternal refuge of those who seek protection from You, carrying us all across the vast ocean of transmigration. Oh cowherd boy, You compassionately shower boons upon Your devotees.

MŪRŪKĀ MŪRŪKĀ VĒL MŪRŪKĀ

Mūrūkā mūrūkā vēl mūrūkā (4x)

O Muruka, son of Shiva and Parvati, You hold the sacred trident in Your hand.

Mūrūkā mūrūkā ena azhaittēn
munvinai yāvūm kalaindaṭuvāy
un ninai vatināl nittamūmē
urūkiṭūm ullam īnṭriṭuvāy nittam

I am calling out, "Muruka, Muruka." O Muruka, remove all of the bad effects of evil actions which are oppressing me. Let my heart over-flow with unbroken remembrance of You.

En manakkōvilil vīttriṭūvāy
eṇṇamkal annaittūm nīkkiṭūvāy
un tirūkkaramkalil aṭiyavanai
ātiṭūm pāvayāy māttriṭūvāy

You reside in the temple of my heart. Dispel all thoughts, please make me a mere puppet in Your divine hands.

Piravā varam tarūm pērazhakā
prāṇava porūlē mālmarukā
pizhaikal porūttū kāttiṭūvāy un
padamalartanil cērttiṭūvāy

O divinely handsome Lord, You bestow the boon of immortality. You are the essence of the eternal mantra, "OM." Please pardon my innumerable faults and misdeeds; grant that I may reach the blessed sanctuary of Your holy feet.

Mūrūkā mūrūkā vēl mūrūkā (4x)
vēl mūrūkā

O Muruka, son of Shiva and Parvati.

NĀM JAPANA KYŌM CHŌḌ

Nām japana kyōm chōḍ diyā
rām nām japana kyōm chōḍ diyā
krōdha na chōḍā jhūṭha na chōḍā
sat vacana kyōm chōḍ diyā

Why did you give up chanting the name, the sacred name of Rama? Without giving up anger and untruth, is it wise to forsake the eternal word?

Jhūṭhē jaga mē dīla lalacākara
asala ratana kyōm chōḍ diyā
kauḍī kō tō khūba sambālā
lāla ratana kyōm chōḍ diyā

Why have you given up the real jewel of the mind and allowed it to crave for sensual objects in the world? You have carefully tended after worthless pebbles, why have you forgotten the red coral?

Jinahī sumirana tē atisukha pāvēm
sō sumirana kyōm chōḍ diyā
khālasa ēka bhagavān bharōsē
tana mana dhana kyōm na chōḍ diyā

By the remembrance of the glories of the Lord one attains to the greatest happiness. Why then have you renounced this blessed remembrance of God? There is only one refuge: it is in God and in faith in Him. Why then don't you abandon this attachment to the body, mind and intellect?

NAMŌ NAMAḤ

Namō namaḥ namō namaḥ
ādi para śakti (4x)

Salutations to the primal supreme power.

Śrī mātā śrī mahārājñī
śrīmat simhāsanēśvarī
cidagnī kuṇḍa sambhūtā
dēvā kārya samudyatā

The Mother of all, the great empress of the whole universe, the sovereign enthroned on a lion's back, who emerged from the fire of pure consciousness, ever promoting the cause of divine forces.

Udyadbhānu sahasrābhā
caturbāhu samanvitā
rāga svarūpa pāśāḍhyā
krōdhā kārāṅkuśōjjvalā
manō rūpēkṣu kōdaṇḍā
pañca tanmātra sāyaka
nijāruṇa prabhāpūra
majjad brahmāṇḍa maṇḍalā

Whose radiance is like a thousand suns rising together, the four-armed divinity. In Your lower left hand You hold a noose representing the power of love. In Your lower right hand You hold the goad of anger for restraining evil forces. You wield the sugar cane bow, representing the mind, in Your upper left hand. And You possess five arrows representing the five subtle elements. In the rosy splendour of Your form, the whole universe is bathed.

Ādi para śakti jay jay ādi para śakti

Victory to the primal supreme power.

NAMŌ NAMASTĒ

Namō namstē mātā saraswati
amṛtamayī ānandamayī
namō namastē nāda śarīriṇi
hamsa vihāriṇi namō namaḥ

Salutations to Saraswati, the Goddess of knowledge, the eternel one, the blissful one. Salutations to the embodiment of sound, whose vehicle is the swan.

Śvetām baradhara keśaghanāmṛta
patmālayarasa manōhari
praṇavamayī satcinmayarūpiṇi
jyōtirmayī tē namō namaḥ

Adorned in white clothes, with thick, black hair. You who are seated upon the Lotus, most beautiful one. The essence of Omkara, the principle of pure existence, enlightened one, salutations to You.

Jñānamayī satgranthamayī śubha
sapta swaramayī namō namaḥ
vīṇā pāṇi suhāmayī mē
dēhi śivam tē namō namaḥ

Embodiment of knowledge, eternal Brahman, foundation of the seven notes of the musical scale, salutations to You. Holding the veena in Your hands, adorned with an enchanting smile, please grant me that which is eternal. My salutations to You.

NANDAKUMĀRA VANDITARŪPA

**Nandakumāra vanditarūpa vṛndāvanabāla
mōhanamuralīgānavilōla gōpīhṛdayēśa
(rādhēśyām)**

O son of Nanda, whose form is worshipped by all, lad of Vrindavan, playing wonderful tunes on the flute, You are the Lord of the hearts of the Gopis.

**Dānavadaityavināśana mādhava
rāsavilōlupa dēvā
nāradatumburusēvitapāda
nārāyaṇa śaraṇam (rādhēśyām)**

Destroyer of demons, husband of Lakshmi, O celestial being, engaged in the rasa lila dance, Your feet alone are worthy to be worshipped by Sages like Narada and Tumburu.

**Janmajarāmṛti saṅkaṭa varjita
santatasukhakara śaurē
vividhābharaṇa vimaṇḍita gātra
vijitākhilahṛdaya (rādhēśyām)**

O Krishna, You are devoid of the suffering of birth, old age and death. O grandson of King Surasena, constant giver of happiness, Your body is decorated with various ornaments; You are the conqueror of all hearts.

**Bhavadaravāraṇa nagavaradhāraṇa
madahara murahara kṛṣṇa
bhāvābhāvavilakṣaṇamāyā-
jālavimōkṣaṇa bhagavan (rādhēśyām)**

O Krishna, You help us to conquer the fears of worldliness. You lifted the great mountain. Destroyer of pride and lust, slayer of the demon, Mura, O Lord, You are the liberator of those trapped in the web of that delusion that is neither existent nor non-existent.

Kālapatē kamalādhipatē
surapālapatē paśujālapatē
bhūmipatē bhuvanādhipatē jaya
sādhupatē sakalādhipatē (nandakumāra)

O Lord of time, Lord of Lakshmi and the Lord of Indra, Lord of all living beings in the universe, Lord of Mother Earth, emperor of the world, victory to the Lord of the Sages, the Lord of everything!

NEÑJAM NIRAINTAVANĒ

Neñjam niraintavanē aṇṇāmalayānē
vañciyōr bhāgam koṇṭa dēvanē
śivanē nī eṅkē śivanē nī eṅkē śivanē nī eṅkē

You who pervade the heart, who reside in Arunachala, O Lord, whose other half is Devi, where are You, O Siva, where are You? O Siva, where are You?

Tañjam un malarppādam aṇṇāmalayānē
mañju tuñjum malai ānavanē

Your lotus feet are our only refuge, You who reside in Arunachala. You are the lofty, snow-covered mountain of Kailas itself.

Kaṭal nañju unṭavanē aṇṇāmalayānē
kātrāki nīrāki analum ānavanē

You consumed the poison which arose when the ocean of milk was churned by the Gods, You who reside in Arunachala. You Yourself are the elements such as the air, the water and the fire.

Piṭṭukka maṇ cumanda aṇṇāmalayānē
pirambaṭi tanaiyum ēttravane

You who carried loads of earth in exchange for rice cake, who reside in Arunachala, You received beatings with a cane for the sake of devotees.

Tiripuram erittavane aṇṇāmalayānē
dīpa oliyāy cuṭarviṭum śivappazhamē

You destroyed the three cities with the fire of Your third eye, You who reside in Arunachala, You are the light of the lamps of Kartika, O Siva, where are You?

Gangayai darittavane aṇṇāmalayānē
kaṇṭavar mayaṅgum aruṭpperum jyotiye

You hold the Ganges river on Your head, You who reside in Arunachala. Everyone who sees You is enchanted. You are the divine light.

NĒTRAṄGALĒ NIṄGAL

Nētraṅgalē niṅgal nēril darśikkuvin
nīraja śyāmala nīla kalebaram
nāsāpuṭaṅgale niṅgal śrīkṛṣṇente
kālttāmarapūmaṇam nukarnnīṭukin

O eyes, you see the real form of Krishna with His dark and curly hair. O nose, you smell the sweet fragrance of His lotus-like feet.

Ṣrōtraṅgale niṅgal ōrkkuvin gōpālā
bālanente vēṇu gānālāpa nisvanam
jīvanōddhāramānāda bījāmṛtam
nāvē svadichālumārtti tīrum varē

O ears, you remember the enchanting music the cowherd boy played on His flute. O tongue, relish the repetition of His name, it is the seed of nectar that uplifts one's life unto complete fulfillment.

Nādānta tīram pravēśikkumātmāvil
omkārabījam muzhaṅgaṭṭe maunamāy
bhāva bhāvātīta bōdha prapañcamā
lāvaṇya lāsyattilāzhaṭṭe sāndramāy

At the far shore of the mind, we enter into our inner Self. There, the sound of Om reverberates in stillness. The manifested and unmanifested universal consciousness serenely resides in its own beauty.

NEYYAPANTAM YĒTRIYA DĪPAM

Neyyapantam yētriya dīpam kaṇdāl
poybandham arupaṭumē idayēśvarī
meibandham nī ēnnum mēnmai koṇdāl
kaibandham kaividumē śivaśankarī

O Goddess of my heart, all of my false attachments fall away when I see the lamp lit for You with pure ghee. All of my worldly ties are severed when I remember that You are the true and only relative.

Ādi guru ānavalē idayēśvarī
ulagellām śivamayam tān śivaśankarī
jyōti rūpa darśanamum idayēśvarī
cholloṇṇā śānti tarum śivaśankarī

Goddess of my heart, You are the first Guru. Shivashankari, everything in this world is Shiva alone. When the vision of You in the form of light is obtained, that vision will bestow supreme peace.

Guru vadivam tānki vantāy idayēśvarī
kuvalayattil telivu tantāy śivaśankarī
tiru vadivum guru vadivum idayēśvarī
arul vadivil ondrāgum śivaśankarī

Goddess of my heart, You have come in the form of the Guru and You have given clarity to the world. Shivashankari, The form of God and the form of the Guru merge in the form of Your grace.

Satguruvē enum śollai idayēśvarī
ceppināl nalam perukum śivaśankarī
śivanāmam anudinamum idayēśvarī
cintikka śivapadam tān śivaśankarī

Goddess of my heart, when the word "Satguru" is chanted it will bring immense benefit. Shivashankari, when the name of Shiva is chanted everyday it takes one to the state of Lord Shiva (liberation.)

NĪLA NĪLA MĒGHA VARṆṆĀ

Nīla nīla mēgha varṇṇā nī varillayō
kuzhalūtiyūti āṭi āṭi nī varillayō
svaramāy layamāy matilayamāy
en maunavīṇa tantri pulki
atiloru rāgadhārayāyuṇarnnu
svaralaya bhāvagāna yamunayāyi
ozhuki varū varū

O You with the color of dark blue clouds, won't You come and play on Your flute and dance? Won't You respond to the silent strings of my veena, awakening sound, melody and rhythm in them? Come, flowing as a divine stream of music, play Your flute and dance an enchanting dance. Come as a dream, as a memory, as inspired music.

Ī manōhara tīraminnum snēhanirbharam
nī pāṭi nirttiyorīṇaminnum bhāvanirbharam
pozhiyu sarasam svaramāriyāyi
nī snēha rāga madhuramāy
kala kala vēṇu gāna lahariyāy
vanapathamāke lāsya naṭanamāṭi
tazhuki varū varū

This beautiful shore resounds with love; the song of Your composition is full of divine inspiration. Come as the beautiful music of the rain, as the sweetness of a love song, as the intoxication of the melody of Your flute. Come dancing gracefully through the forest.

Prēma gāyakanennum nī snēhavāṭiyil
tēn vēṇugānam pāṭiyōmal cōṭuvachiṭum
kanavāy ninavāy nava svanamāy
ī kāvyalōla mānasattil
telimaya tārasundarābha tūki
madhurasa rāgatāla bhāvalahari
vitari varū varū

O minstrel of love, when will You dance to the music of Your flute in this garden of love? Come as a dream, as a memory, as a sweet new sound; come spreading song, music, rythm and the intoxication of divine love in this heart.

NIN MUKHAM KĀṆUMBŌL

Nin mukham kāṇumbōl enmanam telikayay
kaṇṇinu kaṇṇāyorammē
manakkaṇṇinu kaṇṇāyorammē
nin karavalliyālonnu talōṭumbōl
alakaluyarnnīṭunnu śāntitan
alakaluyarnnīṭunnu

O my beloved Mother, my mind brightens when I see Your face. When You caress me with Your soft hands, waves of peace rise up from within me.

Etra janmaṅgalāy yātra ceytinnu ṅān
nin savidhattilaṇaṅṅū
tṛppāda tīrthamaniṅṅū
alayātiniyum evanē dēvi
padataliril cērkkū sadayam
abhayam nīyēkū

After journeying through countless births I have reached You, I have reached Your holy feet. Do not let me wander again, Mother. Let this son rest at Your holy feet. Show mercy and grant refuge.

Karmmatrayaṅgalāl poliyumī jīvitam
karmmaphalam tarum ninakku nalkī
līlānāṭaka ramgam vidhāyinī
aṭi patarunnu ī jīvitasandhyayil
abhayam nalkū nin sēvana caryayil

You who dispense the fruits of action, I give You this life which consists of action. My steps falter now at the twilight of life, please give me refuge at Your side, in Your service.

NINṬRA TIRUKKŌLAM KAṆṬĒN

Ninṭra tirukkōlam kaṇṭēn
nirai tiruppādam kaṇṭēn
anṭralarnda malarai pōla
akam kulirum cirippaikkaṇṭēn

I saw Your standing form, Your adorable, holy feet. I saw You laughing like a freshly blossomed flower that cools the heart.

Uṇṇa nān uṇaveṭuttāl - un
mukham tān atilum kaṇṭēn
enna nān ninaitta pōtum
en amma unai kaṇṭēn

Even when I take food to eat, Your face appears to me in that. Whatever I think about, Mother, I see only You.

Ilaikal asainda pōtum - un
iru vizhikal azhaikka kaṇṭēn
mazhaitulikal vizhunda pōtum - un
manakkaruṇai vellam kaṇṭēn

When leaves blow about it appears as though Your two eyes are calling me. When the raindrops fall it appears to be Your compassion raining down.

Alaikal aṭikka kaṇṭēn
avai karaikul aṭaṅka kaṇṭēn
ārpparikkum entan manamum
annai anpil aṭaṅka kaṇṭēn

I saw the waves on the shore lashing about and then subsiding, just as the restlessness of my mind subsides in the love of my Mother.

ŌM BHADRA KĀLI ŚRĪ BHADRA KĀLI

Ōm bhadra kāli śrī bhadra kāli
jaya bhadra kāli namō namaḥ

Victory to Bhadra Kali, salutations.

Kāli kāli kāli kāli

Prēma sāgari śyāma sundari
bhakti dāyini mukti dāyini

O ocean of compassion, You of a beautiful complexion, You bestow devotion and liberation.

Mātru rūpiṇi prēma rūpiṇi
jay jaga vandini jay jagadīśvarī

Embodiment of the Mother, embodiment of love, the whole world prostrates to You. Victory to the Goddess of the world.

ŌMKĀRA DIVYA PORŪLĒ XIV

Ōmkāra divya porūlē varū
ōmana makkalē vēgam
ōmanayāy valar nāmayaṅgal nīkki
ōmkāra vastuvāy tīru

Come quickly darling children, you who are the divine essence of Om. Remove all sorrows, grow to be adorable and merge with the sacred syllable "Om."

Munnile satguru rūpam ullil
minnunnorātma pratīkam
satguru pādattil cittam ramikukil
attalum baddhalum tīrum

The form of the Guru appearing in front of us is truly a symbol of the Self that shines within us. When our mind revels in the contemplation of the holy feet of the Satguru, all sorrows and struggles will be over.

Mārggam pizhacennu vannāl pinne
lakṣyam pizhaykkāneluppam
mārggalakṣyaṅgal maraññu ninnālasyam
ālunnu lōkayuvatvam

When we miss our way, it is easy for us to miss our goal. Having forgotten both their path and their goal, the youth of the world have fallen into indolence.

Ñān ñānitennōtumārum nēril
ñānā ratārāyvatilla
kālamkozhiyumbōl kōlam poliyumbōl
arōru vārenna satyam

Everyone is always saying, 'I, I', but no one asks what the 'I' really is. When time has suddenly slipped away, and the mortal frame is about to fall off, then who will know the truth of one's real identity?

Svanta dehattil madikum martyan
antakārattil patikum
antakan tīkkaṇṇaruṭṭi mizhikkavē
bandaṅgal ventatu vīzhum

The man who takes pride in his body will fall into darkness. When the Lord of death opens his fiery eyes, all human ties are reduced to ashes.

Poṭṭum poṭiyum perukki naṣṭa
śiṣṭaṅgal tiṭṭa peṭumbōl
satkarmma śudhamām samskāra cittaṅgal
ñaṭṭunnu dharmmakṣayattil

When noble minds, sanctified by good deeds, take stock of the world around them, they are appalled by the rapid decay of virtue.

Kāchi kurukkiya paimbāl klāvu
pātrattil vachāl duṣikum
śuddhīkari kkātta cittil niraykunna
vidyayum vidrōha mākum

Even pure, boiled milk will go bad if kept in an unclean pot. In the same way, the knowledge that is poured into an impure mind will become harmful.

Viṭṭu mārīṭilla nartham manam
keṭṭa mārggattil carichāl
rāgarōgaṅgal madikunnacittattil
vērōṭukillātma śānti

When the mind treads an evil path, there will be no end to misfortunes. The peace of the Self will not take root in a mind in which desire and other worldly ills are rampant.

Citta mālinya makannāl hṛittil
advaita sūyanudikum
bhakti pāthassu koṇṭulam kulirpichu
nitya sāyujyam varikū

When the mind is cleansed of impurities, the light of nondual wisdom will shine forth. Cleanse your hearts with the water of devotion and gain eternal union with the Supreme.

Siddhānta lōkattumātram sthiram
varttikkānāvillorālkum
karttavya śuddhiyum arppaṇa bōdhavum
lakṣhya siddhi kābhikāmyam

No one can remain steadfast in a world governed solely by intellectual spiritual doctrine. Purity of purpose and an attitude of surrender are needed for attaining the goal.

Cittatār melleviṭarnnal svayam
satya pīyūṣam turakum
satguru pādattil sarvam samarpichu
nitya sukhattil ramiku

Gently open the flower of your heart and fill it with the nectar of Truth! Surrender everything at the feet of the Guru and revel in the Truth that is eternal!

Mānava dharmmam ōrāykil manam
hīnam mṛgattine kālum
kāṭāṇu pinne nām kāṇmatellāṭavum
kērikkayarkam ārōṭum

If our minds do not imbibe human virtues, they will be meaner than animal minds. Then we will see a jungle wherever we look, and we will be ready to pick a fight with anyone.

Svantam nizhalōṭu pōlum mṛgam
krōdhichilarikutikum
ghōrakāntāramāy mārum manassine
kāṭaruttārāmam ākū

An animal will pounce on its own shadow and roar in anger! Children, clear the fierce jungle of your own mind and turn it into a garden!

Nālañcu nāl kōṇṭārālkum dharmma
śilam talirkkilla tanne
pārāteceytunām śīlicha śīlaṅgal
mārāneluppam allōrkū

Virtuous habits do not sprout in anyone in four or five days. Remember that it is not easy to change the habits that we have cultivated heedlessly.

Lābha pratīkṣayil mātram śraddha
tuvunnu tāzhunnu cēttil
nilkkān karuttilla kaikāluraykkilla
ettippiṭikunnu mānam

Profit is all we care about and we sink deeper into dirt. We lack the strength to stand up and our feet are not firm. Yet we reach for the sky!

Svārthābhilāṣattoṭoppam tyāga
bōdhavum cērnnu pōvilla
atyanta śaityavum atyuṣṇavum tammil
aikyattil varttikkayilla

Selfish desires do not go hand in hand with renunciation. Extreme heat and extreme cold cannot stay together in the same place.

Mānava lōka svabhāvam kānka
mātsarya buddhikka dhīnam
nōkkilum vākkilum tīkkanalālunnu
terttaṭṭorukunnu krōdham

Know that jealousy holds sway in human nature. There are glowing embers in a man's looks and words. Anger simmers inside a man until he explodes.

Sāmūhya nanmakkiṇakki vyakti
jīvitam samphullamākū
hṛttil vidvēṣavum vākkiladvaitavum
śuddha kāpaṭhyamennōrkū

Make your own life blossom by aligning it with the good of society. Mouthing the principle of nonduality while harbouring spiteful feelings in the heart is the height of deception and hypocrisy.

Svat chandam syōtassu pōle sadā
nirgalichīṭaṭṭe snēham
nalkān kazhiyātta tonnum labhikkilla
eṅgum vitachatēkoyū

Let love flow spontaneously like a fountain. We do not receive anything that we would not give. We only reap what we ourselves sow.

Snēhippatin mānadandham svārtha
lābha pratīkṣayallōrkū
kollal koṭukkalallātma saurabhyamā
ṇulppūviriññazhum snēham

Remember that the basis of love is not the expectation of gaining something. Love is not some form of barter. The love that flows from the blossom of the heart is the fragrance of our real Self.

Nalkuvān onnomillēlum saumya
vākkānnuraykkān kazhiññāl
anyarkkatāśvāsam ēkum dayāmayar
kīśan tannal nalkum ennum

Even if there is nothing else to give, speak a gentle word. That will give solace to others. And the Lord will always shelter those who are compassionate.

Snēhattāl krōdham keṭṭuttām tellum
krōdhattāl krōdham keṭilla
tī koṇṭa tī keṭillālippaṭarnniṭum
nīrvīzhtti vēṇam keṭuttān

Only love can extinguish anger. Anger cannot be put out with more anger. Fire cannot be put out by another fire. The fire will only spread further. We need to pour water in order to put out fire.

Arṣamanassinte mantram ātma
maitritan śamkholi pakṣe
adarśahīnamām asuraśaktikka
tātmāvulaykum ninādam

The mantra of the ancient Sage is the bugle call of love; but, for the unprincipled demonic forces, it is a sound that makes the heart tremble.

Yuddham jayikkāneluppam manō
yuddham jayikkān prayāsam
samyamam śāntidam eṅkilum nirddaya
śaktitan nērkatu vajraṁ

It is easy to win an external battle but hard to win the battles of the mind. Restraint gives peace, but when turned against a ruthless power, it becomes a fierce weapon.

Āśissarulunna nāvāl śāpa
vākyaṅgalōtilla pakṣe
garvitō chīrṣatte mānikkayilla nām
prānan ṇarambil uṭikke

The tongue that speaks words of blessing does not usually utter curses. But as long as there is life pulsating in our body, we would not bow to a head held high in haughtiness.

Mandākinīnadam pōle mantra
sāndramīyārṣa hṛdantam
pāpanāśatti nī pārinte makkalku
bhāvukānugrahatīram

The heart of this ancient land is as saturated with the divine name as the banks of the holy river Ganges are saturated with divinity. It holds out, to all the people of the world, the promise of deliverance from all sins.

Lōka vibhūtikal nēṭām bhōga
lālasarāmyaru tārum
iṣṭa vastukkalōṭoṭṭi ninnulkkalum
niṣprabhamākkaru tārum

You may acquire worldly riches, but do not indulge excessively. Do not take away the glow of your heart by being too attached to objects of desire.

Svapnaṅgal mithyayennālum svapna
kālattu satyamāytōnnum
kāṇunnatellāma nityamennākilum
kāṇunnanērattu satyam

Dreams are unreal but appear real when we are dreaming. Everything that we see is unreal but appears real to our senses.

Ārtta janakṣēma karmmam svantam
kīrttiku vēṇṭiyākāte
karttavyamāy kaṇṭa nuṣṭhikkaṇam mukti
sidhikka tuttama mārggam

Work that alleviates the suffering of others must never be done to enhance one's own fame. See selfless work as one's duty. Then it is the best path to liberation.

Snēhōṣmalam sāra vākum tyāga
bhāvōjvalam lōla hṛttum
sāmuhyananmaykku nēdicha jīvita
bhāvanāśuddhiyum kāmyam

Words of advice filled with the warmth of love, a soft heart glowing with the spirit of sacrifice, a life that is sanctified by being dedicated to the welfare of the society, these are things we should wish for.

Bhāvātmakam mānavaikyam hṛttil
ātmīya śānti varṣikē
nōkilum vākkilum mātram allādrata
vāykum pravṛttiyilellām

When the heart is filled with peace from embracing the ideal of the unity of mankind, then not only one's words and looks but also all of one's actions will become full of the beauty and joy of compassion.

Anpezhātulla manassu cēttil
aṇṭukiṭakunna bhēgam
tyāgam sahikān karuttezhātulavar
kkārukalpikum mahatvam

A loveless heart is like a frog lying immersed in dirt. Who will ascribe greatness to anyone who does not have the strength to undergo any sacrifice?

Snēham svakārya svattalla hṛttil
sāra samajjasa śakti
nirggalichīṭaṇam eṅgumanagalam
keṭṭininnāl keṭṭupōkum

Love is not anyone's private wealth. It is the true binding force of the heart. It should flow out unhindered. It will die if left to stagnate inside.

Pūmaṇam pērippulachu kulir
korittarikunna kāttāy
bhaktipīyūśam nukarnnāttu saurabham
cuttum parattuvin makkal

Children, drink the nectar of devotion and spread the fragrance of the Self. Be like the breeze that is ecstatic from the floral scents it bears and that spontaneously spreads coolness and fragrance around.

Vyaktiyil bandhichitāte śraddha
sattayil bandhikka makal
buddhi māndyam koṇṭu vyakti bandhaṅgalil
sattaye bandhichiṭolle

Children, do not value attachment to other individuals. Bind yourselves to the inner essence. Do not create bondage for yourself out of ignorance by attachment to others.

Dharmma sārārtham grahikkān nūru
grantham paratēṅda makal
svantam manassinte kaṇṇāṭiyil nōkki
entum grahikkān paṭhikū

You do not need to search through a hundred books to grasp the essence of a righteous life. Learn by looking into the mirror of your own mind.

Naśvara bhōgam kotichāl ārum
akṣara sāram grahikkā
klēśichunēṭēṅgatīśvara ajñānamān
āvaradanam varēṇyam

If you crave for transitory pleasures you cannot learn the truth of the Immutable. It is the knowledge of God that you should strive for. That is the greatest boon.

Ujjvalippikuvin makkal hṛttil
advaita śānti caitanyam
mōkṣattinum sarvanāśattinum hētu
cētassil bhāvāntaraṅgal

Kindle in your heart the peace and radiance of oneness with the Supreme. The varying disposition of the heart can be responsible either for salvation or for total ruin.

Kaṇṇalla kāṇunnatonum kēlkum
kātalla kēlkunna tonnum
kāzhcayum kēzhviyum nalkunna śakti tan
ātma caitanya prakāśam

It is not the eye that sees anything. Nor is it the ear that hears anything. The power that enables seeing and hearing is the radiant Self within.

Munpē kutikunu mōham mṛtyam
pinpēyaṭukunnu ghōram
āyussoṭuṅgunna torāte bhōgaṅgal
aśichu nētannu śōkam

Desire springs forward, but death is catching up from behind. Man courts grief by seeking pleasures, unmindful of the fact that life is ebbing away.

Dharmmātma kāmaṅgalellām lakṣya
mūnnunnatātmaikya lābham
kāmārtha mātra prasakkarāyāl phalam
śōkāntakāramā ṇārkum

The traditional objects of life such as wealth, enjoyment and duty are meant to lead to the fourth goal, salvation. If we become engrossed in enjoyment alone, the result will be the darkness of sorrow.

Karmmaṅgal pūjaychāy kaṇdāl phalam
pūjā prasādamāy tirum
jīvitam yajñamāy māttum vivēkikal
nēṭum puruṣārtha lābham

If we offer all actions as worship then the fruits of those actions will be prasad, the sanctified remains of the offering of which we may partake. The wise one who turns life itself into a sacrificial offering attains the goal.

Manniṭam mānichiṭāte svargga
sannidhi tēṭunnu kaṣṭam
muṭṭitturakkēṇṭavātilariyāte
muṭṭiyālāruturakam

Alas, man searches for heaven without paying respect to life here on Earth. If we don't know which door to knock on, who will answer our knock?

Ōrātirikkavē daivam ēre
dūre yāṇennorttu pōkum
ōrukil cārattā ṇānandasāram tan
cētasil caitanya dhāmam

In our ignorance, we imagine that the Lord is far away. Upon attaining real knowledge we will see that He is nearby. He is the essence of bliss, the Self within our heart.

Īśvara prēmattin munnil vyakti
snēhaṅgalellām nissāram
kuññinotammaykkezhunna snēhattilum
nirmmala māṇatin bhāvam

The love amongst ourselves is nothing when compared to God's love for us. The Lord's love is purer than a mother's love for her child.

Tēṭuvin makkalē niṅgal satya
lōkam svayam svanta hṛttil
pāṭuvin makkalē daiva saṅkīrttanam
nēṭukā pādāravindam

Search for the world of Truth in your own heart, children!
Sing the divine name and search for His lotus feet!

Arppitacētasilennum sargga
raśmikal narttanam ceyyum
vyaktatayārnniṭum jīvita rathya
pinnīśvara prēmābhiṣēkam

The rays of divine light will dance in the heart that is surrendered to Him and will illumine the path of life. Such a heart will be awash with divine love.

ŌM NAMŌ NAMAḤ ŚIVĀYA

Ōm namō namaḥ śivāya (4x)

Salutations to Lord Shiva.

Sarvva mantra yantra mūrtti
ādi śrī gurō namaḥ
tṛppādāmbujam tozhunnu
sarvvamangalattināy

Prostrations to the Lord of all mantras and all yantras, the first in the line of Gurus. I bow to Your lotus feet, repository of all auspiciousness.

Ādhi vyādhināśanam
sudhāmayam cinmayā
klēśabharita jīvitattil
ēkunī kṛpādhanam

Lord, in this life full of misery, grant me the treasure of Your compassion, the nectar which dispels darkness and disease.

Kāmadam mōkṣadam
sarvvasiddhi dāyakam
bhavakāraṇa mṛtikāraṇa tanumbōdhamakattaṇam

Fulfill my wishes, grant me liberation and give me all the siddhis. Remove my body sense, which is the cause of the grief of samsara.

Saprabham asamga
satchidānandam advayam
ahamitennurachasvānu
bhutiyāṇannugraham

The direct experience that I am none other than the Self-effulgent, (asamga), Satchidananda, is the blessing that I seek from You.

Śiva śiva śiva (3x) śaṇkara
hara hara hara (3x) abhayamkara
śiva śiva śiva śaṇkara pārvati paramēśvarā

Giver of refuge, O Shiva and Parvati.

ORU MANDIRAM ARIYA

Oru mandiram ariya tiru mandiram
śaravaṇa bhava eṇum aru mandiram
ata tantiṭum palanil sukham kaṇṭiṭum
gati vandiṭum nalla vazhi tōnṭiṭum

"Sharavana Bhava" (Lord Subramanyan) is the one mantra that is rare. It gives lasting happiness, leads to higher states and opens up an auspicious path.

Alaikinṭra manatirkku amaitiyai tantiṭum
anaivarkkum potuvākum arumandiram
nōvukku maruntāki nontārkka tuṇayāki
nāvukkul ninṭrāṭi nalam śērttiṭum

This divine mantra gives peace to restless hearts like the balm for pain. It is the only refuge for those in agony. Those who chant this mantra reap great benefits.

Piravippiṇitīra pillaikku maruntīyum
perumān nī emkalatu perumaruttuvan
turavi ēnum kolattum tuya piravaṭivattum
tunbankal nīmkīṭa tuṇai vandiṭum

O Lord, You are our great physician who gives medicine for the disease of birth and death. Your mantra is the only help for the sannyasins as well as others to overcome their grief.

Vēl vēl murukā vetri vēl murukā
śakti vēl murukā jñāna vēl murukā

O Muruka, who holds the spear, You are the embodiment of divine energy and eternal knowledge.

ORU MANDIRAM ATA

Oru mandiram ata tirumandiram
ōm amṛtēśvaryai namaḥ enum mandiram

The great mantram, "Om Amriteshwaryai Namah," is holy and sacred.

Atai eṇṇuvōr neñcam sukham kaṇṭitum
gati vandiṭum nal vazhi tōnṭriṭum

The hearts of those who meditate on this mantra rejoice, and the spiritual path beckons them.

Piravippiṇi tīrkka pillaikka marundīvāy
pēdai enaikkākka viraintōṭi vāray
nōvukka marundānāy nōndārkka tuṇaiyānāy
nāyēnukkanaittum nalkiṭum tāyānāy

O Mother, give me the medicine to cure this cycle of birth and death, come fast to save this ignorant child of Yours. You are the cure for all maladies and the refuge for broken hearts. You are the Mother who showers me with all good things.

Ōrāyiram nāmam ōrāyiram - manam
ōyāmal tuti pāṭum un gītam

O Mother, You have thousands and thousands of names. Let my mind praise Your glory forever.

Nondiṭum enaittēṭra tāmadam eni ēnō
sondamena azhaittēn tāyē manam kanivāy
kaṭaikkaṇ pāramma kavalaikal tīrammā
aṭaikkalam enṭrum un tiruppādam ammā

Why do You hesitate to console this suffering child? I called to You as the only relation in this world for me. Hearing this call, won't Your heart melt? Glance at me, Mother, and remove all obstacles. Your holy feet are the only solace and support for this one.

Ōrāyiram nāmam ōrāyiram - manam
ōyāmal tuti pāṭum un gītam

O Mother, You have thousands and thousands of names. Let my mind praise Your glory forever.

Amṛtānandamayī abhayapradāyini
akhilāṇḍēśvarī ānandarūpiṇi

Embodiment of immortal bliss, who grants protection, Goddess of the universe, of blissful form.

ORU MŌHAMINNITĀ

Oru mōhaminnitā ammē
eriyunnennullil aniśam
oru mātram nīyennilammē
kanivin mizhittellaṇaykkū

O Mother, a desire is burning within me constantly; won't You cast Your compassionate glance upon me, even for just one moment?

Parayuvān āvatill ammē - tellum
nirayunnu vēdana mātram
arivilla pātayum munnil - itā
irularnnu sandhya yiṅgetti

I cannot describe even a small amount of the sorrow that fills me. I do not know the path before me, dusk has come and the sky grows dark.

Piṭayunnu prāṇanī kūṭṭil - kaṣṭam
veṭiyola nīyī vidhattil
noṭi nēram vaikarutammē - vannu
maṭiyāte vāriyaṇaykkū

My life is fluttering within this cage of the body. Please do not forsake me like this. Do not delay even for a moment. Come and take me into Your arms without delay.

Pariyolla nīyenne viṇṭum - ammē
parayū nī vaikunnatente
nirabhakti dīpam telichan - manam
arivinte śrī kōvilākkū

Do not leave me stranded like this, separated from You. O Mother, why this delay? Lighting the lamp of radiant love, convert my mind into the temple of knowledge.

Tirumāril oru pon maṇi - pōl
tarukī makaninnabhayam
tiruppāda pūjā malarāy - nityam
viṭaraṭṭe jīvita sūnam

Grant me shelter, like a jewel adorning Your radiant form. Let the flower of this life blossom as an offering of worship at Your holy feet.

Ō VĀSUDĒVĀ

Ō vāsudēvā paṇindōm mukundā
kuzhandaikal azhaittōm viraindōṭi vāräy
giritanai viral tannil ēndiya bālā
tunpachumaikalai tāṅkiyē vandōm

O Krishna, Vasudeva, we pray to You, Mukunda, who bestow Liberation. Your children call for You, do come fast. To You, the little one, who carried even a great mountain on Your finger, we come with the large burden of our sorrows.

Kanindarul tārāy
kavalaikal tīrppāy
manakkōvil tanilē
vītriḍa vārāy

Bestow Your grace to us and end our woes, come and reside in the temple of our mind.

Āzhnda nal anpinai
kāṇikkai tandōm
ā nirai mēyppavanē
āṇṭarul tārāy

We give our deep and our pure love as our only offering, O the herder of cows, bless us with victory.

Vandiṭa iniyum
tāmatam ēnō
vaṇaṅkiṭum āṭiyavartam
manatil olirpavanē

Why do You delay in coming? What is the reason? You shine in the hearts of all who surrender to You.

Gōpālā kṛṣṇā śrī hari kṛṣṇā
gōvinda kṛṣṇā rādhē kṛṣṇā

O Krishna, cowherd boy, Lord of the cows, Lord of Radha.

PĀDAMŪLATTILE PĀMSUVĀY

Pādamūlattile pāmsuvāy māttumō
pāvanē nīyenneyammē
kōṭiviśvaṅgalkku tāyē orikkalī
ēzhayēyōrkkumō cite? ī
ēzhayēyōrkkumō cittē

When will I become the dust on Your lotus feet? O Holy Mother, won't You grant me this? O Mother of infinite worlds, just for once, won't You remember this helpless child?

Viśvam camaykkunna nin vīkṣaṇam verum
nissāranāmennil vīnāl
ānanda dhāmamām nin pādam pūkuvān
ñānum samartthanākillē? ammē
ñānum samartthanākillē?

If only Your glance, powerful enough to create universes, should fall on this insignificant one, won't I be able to reach Your blessed feet, the abode of bliss.

Nin mukhābhōjam pozhikkunna puñchiri-
ppūnilāvennil patichāl
śōkatāpaṅgal śamichennilamba nin
prēmam niraññīṭukillē? bhakti
bhavam niraññīṭukillē?

If the effulgent moonbeams of Your sweet smile, emanating from Your radiant face, should fall on me, then won't my sorrows vanish and the buds of devotion blossom in me?

Nīyenneyōrkkukil dhanyanāyannu ñān
nīyonnu nōkkukil muktan
nin padāntēyaṇachiṭumōyenne nī
nin prēmamēkumō tāyē? ennil
nin prēmamēkumō tāyē?

If You remember me I am blessed; if You glance at me I am freed. Won't You draw me to Your side, won't You shower me with Your love, Mother, won't You shower me with Your love?

PĀDĀRAVINDHANGAL

Pādāravindhangal paṇindhēn ammā
ādhāram nī endru arinthen ammā
chedāram illāmal chezhippai thandhu
kādhoram inmozhiyāl kavalai thīrppāi

Mother, I bow to Your feet. I have realized that You are the foundation of my life. Give me the wealth that can never be depleted. Whisper sweetly in my ear and end my sorrows.

Ammā endrazhaikkum un kuzhanthaikku inghe
arulandri vērēthuvum vēndām ammā
summā nī inimēlum irunthu viṭṭāl
pazhi yēdhum yenakkalla unakkē ammā

O Mother, wanting nothing except Your grace, this child of Yours is calling, 'O Amma! Amma!' If you still remain silent then remember, Mother, You will be the one to blame, not I.

Selvangal yerālam irunthālum un
arul selvam illāmal nargahti undō
inbathil pangerka evarum varuvāy
ennālum thuyar thīrka nīyē varuvāy

Though we may have much worldly wealth, could we ever attain the one true end without the wealth of Your grace? There are always many to share in our happiness, but You are always the only one who removes my sorrow.

Ellām un vilayādal ena arinthālum
enō yen manathil innum nimmadhi illai
thunbam varumbhōthum maravathunnāi
manamāra pōtrum nal ullam vēndum

I know that all this is but Your play and yet my mind knows no peace. Please bestow upon me a mind that remembers and glorifies You even when suffering comes.

PANNAGĀBHARAṆA

Pannagābharaṇa paśupatē
pavalavāy maṇiyē umāpatē
cinmaya rūpā paśupatē
cintayil varuvāy umāpatē

O Lord Pasupati (Shiva), bedecked with snakes, O precious Lord with ruby red lips, You are the embodiment of consciousness. Please grace my thoughts, O Lord of Uma.

Pādapamkajam paṇintiṭuvōm
padamalar sernthida tutittiṭuvōm
vēdattin āzhnta karuttukalin
vilankum uyirai nāyakanē

We bow down to Your lotus feet and pray to merge in that. O Lord, You shine as the essence of the scriptual truths.

Anaithilum irukkum paramporulē
adiyarkamudhām adaikkalame
meniyil pādhiyai pakirndhavane
inimai taruvāy śankaranē

O eternal Lord, You are present in everything. You are the eternal refuge for the devotees. You gave away half of Your body (to Parvati). Please bless us with all that is sweet, O auspicious one.

Unainān māravan varam alippai
ulamtanil sudar vidum oli vilakke
unnil irandara nānkalakka
uṭanē vandu arul purivāy

Please give me the boon that I may never forget You. You are the one that shines as the divine light in the mind. Please bless me to)merge in You without delay.

PASIYENTRĀL UṬAN

Pasiyentrāl uṭan
rusiyamudāvāy ammamma
naṭu nisiyentrāl uṭan
nilavāy varuvāy ammamma

O Amma, when I suffer from hunger You come as a sumptuous meal. On a dark night, You come as the moonlight.

Nāvularntāl uṭan
taṇṇīrāvāy ammamma
indha nāniluṁ varaṇṭāl māri
entrāvāy ammamma

When I am thirsty, You come as a drink of water. When this Earth is dry, You come as the rain.

Nān vizhuntāl uṭan tānkiṭa
varuvāy ammamma
ennil nānezhuntāl uṭan āṇavaṁ
aṭakkuvāy ammamma

If I happen to fall down, You rush to pick me up. If my ego rises up then You immediately remove it.

Nān azhutāl uṭan
ārutal solvāy ammamma
inku nān siritthāl uṭan
sintanai seyvāy ammamma

When I cry You console me, when I laugh You think of me.

Nān seyuṁ vinaikalai
kaṇakkinil eṭuppāy ammamma
atai nankukka nārpatāy
tiruppi koṭuppāy ammamma

You add up all of my actions and give me multifaceted results.

PAṬI PUKAZHTTUVĀN

Paṭi pukazhttuvān āvillenikku nin
pāvana jīvita prābhavaṅgal
bhāvōjjvalaṅgalām gītaṅgal pōlum nin
prēma prapañcattilartha śūnyam

I am unable to adequately sing the praises of Your pure and glorious life. Even the most devotional and resplendent of songs appears meaningless and empty before Your universal love and compassion.

Ārente prāṇanil spandichu mēvunnu
ārenne ñānākki nirttiṭunnu
ārenmanassinte ārāmavāṭiyil
ānandanṛtam caviṭṭiṭunnu

You are the substratum of the power of life; from You my being arises. Within my mind, You dance freely.

Āgamam pāṭippukazhttunnatāreyā
ṇārilī viśvam viriññunilpū
ārīyulakinnuyirēki jīvante
ādyattuṭippāril ninnutirnnu

It is for You that the scriptures sing their praises. This world has bloomed forth from You who gave it life. You are the supreme soul of all souls.

Lōkattin uṇmayām ammahā śaktiyen
ammayā enpārnnavatarichu
āyiram neyvilakkētti veykkām
dalamāyiramulla patmattilennum

From that supreme energy, the source of all life, have You incarnated as Mother. I will light one thousand ghee filled lamps of worship in the thousand-petaled lotus of my soul.

Viśvam vilakkum prakāśamūrtte hṛttil
advaita vidyā viśiṣṭa murttē
arkkānalādi prapañcavittē śuddha
cinmātra sattē namō namastē

The embodiment of the light of the world, the only truth and knowledge, the most priceless of pearls, the sun, fire and the seed of the universe, who manifested from pure consciousness, I salute You.

Kālkal praṇāmaṅgal arppikkeyānanda
bāṣpārdram ākunnitantaramgam
mātāmṛtēśvarī sūrya tējōmayī
nī tānulakinnorātma bandhu

While prostrating at Your blessed feet, my mind melts with tears. O, immortal Goddess, in this world You are all that is dear to this soul.

PĀVANI DAYĀKARI

Pāvani dayākari dēvi dēhi mamgalam
pāhi pāhi śrīkari virāgiṇi purātani
śāmbhavi śivamkari sadāviśuḍharūpiṇi
śāśwati jaganmayī sanātani suhāsini

O holy one, You who shower compassion on all, O Goddess, bestow auspiciousness. Please protect me, bestower of prosperity, detached one, ancient one. O Shambavi, engaged in uplifting, auspicious deeds; of perpetually pure form, eternal one, You who pervade the whole world, O everlasting one, endowed with a beautiful smile.

Jaya bhavāni jaya mahēśī
jaya suvāṇi śankari

Victory to Bhavani, victory to the great Goddess, whose speech is sweet, the auspicious one.

Bhārati himādriputri
śōbhanē vimōhini
sarvadukhahāriṇi
garvamūlanāśini

O Bharati, daughter of the Himalayas, O effulgent one, enchantress, You dispel all sorrows and uproot the ego.

Sāmagānavādini
mātṛrūpadhāriṇi
mālini manōpahāra
ghōra māravāriṇi

You are the one who revels in the hymns of the Sama Veda, who assumes the form of the Mother, O Goddess Durga, You are the destroyer of the lust that consumes the mind.

POṬṬIKKARAÑÑU

Poṭṭikkaraññu karaññu ñān ammatan
pādē layikunna dinamennahō
enna parādhaṅgal sarvvam poruttenne
nin padē cerkunna dinamennahō
amṛtēśvarī ammē jagadambikē

I burst out crying and crying. When will dawn that day when I become totally immersed in Your blessed feet? When is that day when, forgiving all my foolish sins, I will become completely dissolved into Your path?

Ninpāda sarattin muttāyirunnemkil
nin pāda dhvatikal kēṭṭēnē
nin pāda dhvanikal ñāṇ eppazhum kēṭṭente
pāpaṅgalellām tīrnnēnē
samastā parādam poruttīṭaṇē

nin pāda patmē cērttīṭaṇē
amṛtēśvarī ammē jagadambikē

If I were a bead in Your anklet, I would hear Your each and every footstep. Listening thus, forever, to the melody of Your footsteps, all my sins would be washed away. Bearing all my sins, immerse me in Your sacred feet, eternal Goddess, universal Mother.

Nin pādapatmē layichoru mānasam
prāptamayīṭān kotikunnu ñān
ennile ājñānamakavē mutinī
nin tirupādattil cērttīṭaṇē
samastāparādham poruttīṭaṇē
ninpādapatmē certtīṭaṇē
amṛtēśvarī ammē jagadambikē

I long to become established in that mind which has totally dissolved into Your immaculate feet. Destroying all the ignorance of my heart, make me one with those feet. Bearing all my sins, immerse me in Your sacred feet, eternal Goddess, universal Goddess.

PRĒMA KĀ DĪPA JALĀ DŌ

Prēma kā dīpa jalā dō
tērī smaraṇā mē magna karā dō
mērē prabhu hē dayā nidhān
mērē bhagavān jay śrī rām

O Lord, light the lamp of love in my heart, let me be immersed in Your remembrance. O my Ram, embodiment of kindness, victory to You.

Bhaṭaktā hē man dukha dētā hai
tuchasē dūr kahī lē jātā hai
kṛpā karō mērē rām (2x)
mana mandira mē karnā tu vas

As my mind is always wandering, it gives me nothing but sorrow. It takes me far away from You. Please have compassion on me, shower Your mercy in the temple of my heart.

Na ātā hē gīt na sur sajtā hai
rām, hē rām, kahnā ātā hai
kṛpā karō mērē rām
tērē darshan ki hē chāhat ram

I don't know any songs, nor do I know how to sing properly. I only know how to call out Your name. My dear Ram, bestow Your grace upon me.

Kṛpā karō mērē rām
prēma kā dīpa jalā dō āj

O my Lord Ram, bestow Your grace and light the lamp of love in my heart today.

PRĒMA KĪ AGAN HŌ

Prēma kī agan hō
bhakti sagan hō
man mē lagan hō tō
prabhu mil jāyēmgē (2x)

If the fire of love is alight and one is full of divine love, if one dedicates one's mind and heart to the supreme, then the Lord shall be attained.

Hṛdaya mē bhāv hō

anunay kī chāv hō
arādhan kā khāv hō tō
man khil jāyēmgē (2x)

If the heart is full of love and one is humble and does everything in a spirit of worship, then the mind shall blossom.

Śraddhā kī jyōt hō
manmē na khōṭṭ hō
karuṇā kā śrōt hō tō
prabhu śrī āyēmgē (2x)

If there is the light of sraddha and the mind is pure, if one is endowed with compassion, then the Lord shall come.

Caraṇōm kī chāh hō
bhakti pravāh hō
puja kī rāh hō tō
prabhu harshayēmgē (2x)

If there is devotion to the Lord's holy feet and if there is a flow of bhakti, if one adopts the path of worship, then the Lord shall be pleased.

Bhajanōmkē bōl hō
bhāv anumōl hō
archan kē mōl hō tō
prabhu muskurayēmgē (2x)

If one sings bhajans with devotion and if one is endowed with the wealth of dedication to the Lord then the Lord shall smile.

Nārāyaṇ dhan hō
cavimē magan hō
archan bhandhan hō tō
prabhu darshayēmgē (2x)

If one is blessed with a devoted heart and is enchanted by the divine form of the Lord, if one worships the Lord with love, the Lord shall reveal Himself.

PRĒMA MĒ JIYŌ

Prēm mē jiyō amṛt piyō
prēm mē jiyō ānand mē rahiyō

Live in love and drink the nectar of inner bliss. Live in love and be happy.

Prēm kī dēvi kī jaya jaya bōlō
parāśakti kī jay jay bōlō

Salutations to the Goddess of love and ultimate power.

Prēm kē sāgar sē jō tēr jāyē
māyā kē jāl mē vō phas jāyē
prēm kē sāgar mē jō ḍūb jāyē
amṛt pīyē amar ban jāyē

One who swims away from the ocean of love gets caught in the net of illusion. But the one who drowns in the ocean of love drinks the nectar of bliss and becomes immortal.

Dēvi kō jō harānā cāhē
uskī hār avaśya hō jāyē
hār kē sab kuch jō ā jāyē
uskī vijay avaśya hō jāyē

One who defies the Goddess will certainly face defeat. But one who approaches the Goddess with an attitude of helplessness will surely find victory.

Prēm kī dēvi kī jay jay bōlō
parāśaktī kī jay jay bōlō

prēm sē bōlō jay jay bōlō
sab mil bōlō jay jay bōlō

Salutations to the Goddess of supreme love and ultimate power. Sing Her praises with love, sing Her praises together!

Prēm kī dēvi prēm kī rānī
prēm svarūpiṇi sab kuch hamāri

Goddess of love, queen of love, embodiment of love, You are our all-in-all.

RĀDHA TAN SANDĒŚAM

Rādha tan sandēśam ettī mathurayil
kaṇṇaniṅgōṭṭonnu vannīṭaṇē
ennuṭe vīṭṭil varēṇṭa sakhē
vṛndāvanattilēkkettīṭaṇē

Radha's message reached Mathura: "O Krishna, please come just once! You need not come to my house and visit me, but, I pray, come to Vrindavan at least!"

Kālindītīram kaṭambin cuvaṭṭilāy
kāṇumoru kochu śavakuṭīram
kaṇṇante dāsiyennuṇṭām phalakavum
pullum karīlayum mūṭī mīte

There You will see a small tomb under a kadamba tree, on the banks of the Yamuna. This humble servant of Yours will be in it, Kanna, under a covering of grass and leaves.

Ākuṭīrattil nī kālonnu cērkkukil
kṛṣṇā kṛṣṇā ennu kēlkkumallō
rādhā śarīrattin ōrō kaṇaṅgalum
nāmam japikkunna nādamallō

If You put Your ear to the tomb, You will hear 'Krishna! Krishna!' being chanted. That is the sound of every atom of Radha's body repeating Your name.

En kuṭīrattil nin kaṇṇil ninnum raṇṭa
kaṇṇir kaṇaṅgal patichītumō
ninne ninachuninchumarichīṭum
rādhaykkuvēronnum vēṇṭa kaṇṇā

Will two drops of tears fall on my tomb from Your eyes? Radha, who is dying with only You in her thoughts, wants nothing else, Kanna!

RĀDHĒ KṚṢṆĀ (GŌPIKĀ RAMAṆA)

Rādhē kṛṣṇā rādhē kṛṣḥṇā rādhē rādhē
rādhē kṛṣṇā rādhē kṛṣṇā rādhē rādhē
kṛṣṇā rādhē rādhē

Gōpikā ramaṇā kṛṣṇā gōkulabālā
mōhana rūpā kṛṣṇā nīla śarīrā
kuñjavihārā kṛṣṇā mañjulapādā
sundaravadanā kṛṣṇā rañjitalōkā

O enchanter of the Gopis, O Krishna of enchanting form and blue complexion, who sports along the groves of Vrindavan, endowed with beautiful feet and a handsome face, You charm the whole world.

Kisalaya caraṇā kṛṣṇā kuvalaya nayana
śaśi samavadana kṛṣṇā mṛdupadanaṭana
mṛdumṛduhasitā kṛṣṇā madhumayavacanā
munimanaharaṇa kṛṣṇā śubhaśatanilaya

Whose feet are as soft as a tender leaf, O lotus-eyed one, Your face shines like the radiant moon. You dance softly, O Krishna. With a charming smile and nectarous words, You captivate the hearts even of great Sages. You are the abode of hundreds of virtues.

Dēvakitanayā kṛṣṇā kāliyadamanā
kalimalaśamanā kṛṣṇā śubhamayacaritā
natajanaśaraṇā kṛṣṇā bhava bhayaharaṇā
janimṛtiśamanā kṛṣṇā śivavidhivinutā

O son of Devaki, subjugator of Kaliya, You who remove the impurities of this dark age of materialism, whose tale is auspicious, O Krishna, the refuge of those who surrender to You, the dispeller of the fear of transmigration, who liberate us from the cycle of births and deaths, even Shiva and Brahma bow down to You.

RĀDHĒ RĀDHĒ GŌVINDA

Rādhē rādhē Gōvinda
bhajō rādhē rādhē gōpālā (2x)

Worship Radha and Krishna, the Lord of the cows, the cowherd boy.

Rādhā lōlā Gōvinda
rāsa vilōlā gōpālā
rādhā rañjana Gōvinda
ramaṇiya veṣā gōpālā

The lover of Radha, Lord of the cows, who danced in the rasa leela, cow herd boy, who pleases Radha, endowed with a most pleasing form.

Nanda mukundā Gōvinda
navanita cōrā gōpālā
kāliya mardhana Gōvinda
kaustubha bhūṣaṇa gōpālā

The giver of happiness, Lord of the cows, the stealer of butter, cowherd boy, the slayer of Kaliya, adorned by the Kaustubha gem.

Vēṇu vilōlā Gōvinda
vijaya gōpālā gōpālā
Gōvinda jaya Gōvinda
gōpālā jaya gōpālā

Who is ever fond of the flute, Lord of the cows, victorious cow herd boy, Salutations to You.

RĀGA VAIRIKAL NIṄGITUM

Rāga vairikal niṅgitum
duritāmayaṅgaloṭuṅgitum
mānasam bhava śōka tāriṇī
ammayil vilayikkukil

If the mind merges in the Mother, the dispeller of all of the sorrows of the world, then all of the foes in the form of desires will vanish and all sorrows and miseries will disappear.

Kanmaṣaṅgalakanna pōyatumuṇ
matan nila vanniṭum
cinmayī tvayī santatam mama
cintayōkkeyaṭaṅgaṇē

The sinful shadows of the heart will lift, one will abide in the Truth. O embodiment of consciousness, may my thoughts subside forever.

Khinnataykku virāma miṭṭatha
bhinnabhāvamakattaṇē
dhanyamāy varumeṅkilījani
manmanō sukha kārini

Will You put an end to my sorrows and remove my feeling of separateness? Then this birth of mine will be fulfilled. O Mother, You are the giver of bliss in my mind.

Tāpanāśaka tāvakāmṛtha
hāsamennil tūvukil
āśapāśa maruttu ñān tava
śānti dhāmam aṇaññiṭum

Remover of sorrows, if You grace me with Your nectarous smile, breaking the bonds of desire I will reach the far shore of eternal peace.

RĀMACANDRAM MANŌBHIRĀMAM

Rāmacandram manōbhirāmam
jaya jānakī prabhum vandēham
bōdhānta bhāsura bhāva pradīptam
saumya svabhāvam nijānanda rūpam

Salutations to Lord Rama, the Lord of Janaki (Sita), who is effulgent with the light of supreme consciousness. Soft and compassionate in nature, He is the embodiment of the bliss of the Self.

Sahasrēndu sadṛśa mukhāravindam
dūrvādala śyāma sumōhana rūpam
śiva maralumā nayanayugam
arkkēndu maṇdhalam ādhāradhāmam

I salute Lord Rama who has a face full of the beauty of a thousand moons and a body with a captivating dark complexion, whose eyes bestow auspicious blessings and who is the source of all.

Vibhum tārakākhyā sudhārasātmā
karuṇārṇṇava hṛdayā harilīla dēvā
tava mandahāsēnu ahamattu nityam
svāntattilanu bhūti surabhilamākāvū

I worship the Supreme Lord, who takes us across the ocean of samsara, who is the bliss of the Self, whose heart is an ocean of compassion. Lord, may Your benign smile bring an end to my ego and fill me with the fragrance of inner bliss.

Harē rāma harē rāma rāma rāma harē harē
harē kṛṣṇā harē kṛṣṇā kṛṣṇā kṛṣṇā harē harē

RĀMACANDRA RAGHUVĪRA

Rāmacandra raghuvīra
rāmacandra rana dhīra

O Lord Rama, of the family of Raghus, brave Lord Rama.

Rāmacandra raghu rāma
rāmacandra param dhāma

Lord Rama, You are the ultimate support and refuge, the final abode for all.

Rāmacandra raghu nāthā
Rāmacandra jagan nāthā

Lord of the Raghus, You are the ruler of the whole world.

Rāmacandra mama bandō
Rāmacandra daya sindō

Lord Rama, You are my own dear friend; You are a river of compassion for all.

Raghu rāma param dhāma

Lord Rama, You are the ultimate refuge.

Raghu nāthā jagan nāthā

Lord of the Raghus, You are the ruler of this world.

Mama bandō daya sindō

You are my friend and You are a river of compassion.

RĀSA VIHĀRĪ

Rāsa vihārī kuñjavihārī
nijajana hṛdaya vihārī
bhava bhaya hārī kaustubha hārī
narakāsura samhārī (2x)

You who enjoy the rasa dance, who play in the groves of Vrindavan, Krishna, You dwell in the hearts of Your devotees. You destroy the fear of worldly existence, O You who wear the kaustubha gem, the slayer of Narakasura.

Sarasijanābha sarasija nētra
sarasīruha mṛdu caranā
sarasijahastā sarasijavadanā
sarōjanī manōramana

You whose eyes shine like a lotus, whose feet are as soft as lotus petals, You with lotus-like hands and face, You make Sarojani (Laksmi) happy.

Madhusūdana hē madhumaya vigraha
madhura smitayutha vadanā
madhubhāṣaṇa hē madhurālāpitā
muralīdhara paśupālā

O slayer of Madhu, O embodiment of sweetness, always endowed with sweet speech, sweet songs and a sweet smile, You are the holder of the flute and the protector of all beings.

Gōpakumārā gōparipālā
gōpījanamana chōra
gōkula nāthā gōpajanēśā
gōvinda jaya vandē

Son of Nanda Gopa, cowherd boy, who steals the mind of all of the Gopis, Lord of Gokul and protector of the cows, victory to You, Govinda, prostrations.

RUṬHĀ HĒ KYŌ MĒRĒ LĀL

Ruṭhā hē kyō mērē lāl
ab tō hasa dē jarā
maiyā kahē sun rē śyām
vraja kā tu hē dūlārā
itanā bōlā bhālā

My darling (Krishna), why have You become so angry? I, Your mother, Yashoda, say that my darling Krishna is the most beloved out of everyone in Vrindavan. Krishna is so sweet and innocent.

Ākē galē lag jā rē kānhā
chōḍ dē yē gussā
kyā maiyā kē hāthō sē
mākhan nahī khānā

ab tō mān lē śyām he
ab tō has dē jarā

O Kanna, come running and embrace me with Your arms around my neck. Leave Your anger behind. Don't You want to eat delicious butter from Your mother's hands? At least now, please relent and give Your mother a smile.

Naṭakhaṭa hē mērā kānhā nahī
kabhī mākhan curāyā nahī
jhūṭh kahē sabhī gvālinē hā (2x)

Who says that my Krishna is a naughty child? He has never stolen butter from the house of the Gopis. What those milkmaids say is totally baseless.

Tu hē mērā nandalālā
mēri ānkhon kā tārā
ītanā hē suṇdara ītanā hē pyāra
sab kē man kō haranē vālā
vraja kā tu hē dulārā

You are the darling of Nanda, my most beloved. My Krishna is so beautiful, so lovely. He is the one who steals all the hearts; He is the darling of Vrindavan.

ŚAKTI DŌ JAGADAMBĒ

Śakti dō jagadambē bhakti dō jagadambē
prēm dō jagadambē mā mujhē
viśvās dēkar rakṣa karō
amṛtēśvarī jagadambē

Divine Mother, give me strength; Divine Mother, give me devotion; Divine Mother, give me pure love; O Divine Mother, protect me by giving me perfect faith, O immortal Goddess, Mother of the universe

Mātē jagadambē māyā tama nāśē
amṛtēśvarī jagadambē mā
dīnāvana śīlē ganāmṛta lōlē
amṛtēśvarī jagadambē mā

O Mother of the universe, destroyer of the darkness of delusion, O compassionate one, You revel in the nectar of song, O immortal Goddess.

Śvētāmbara vasanē nīlāmbuja nayanē
amṛtēśvarī jagadambē mā
sōmōpama vadanē sakalāmaya śamanē
amṛtēśvarī jagadambē mā

O Mother, who is dressed in robes of white, whose eyes are like blue lotus flowers, whose face is as radiant as the full moon, remover of all inauspiciousness, O immortal Goddess, Mother of the universe.

Karuṇā rasa hṛdayē śaraṇāgata varadē
amṛtēśvarī jagadambē mā
śivadāyini śubhadē manamōhini mahitē
amṛtēśvarī jagadambē mā

O Mother, whose heart is filled with the milk of compassion, You grant boons to those who take refuge in You, O giver of auspiciousness, O enchanter of the mind, O great one, O immortal Goddess, Mother of the universe.

Sumanōhara śamanē sukharūpini saumyē
amṛtēśvarī jagadambē mā
lalanāvara rūpē layakāriṇi durgē
amṛtēśvarī jagadambē mā

You move so gracefully, embodiment of well-being, O beautiful one, O divine beloved, O Durga, who grants us oneness, O immortal Goddess, Mother of the universe.

SAMASTA PĀPANĀŚANAM (VIṢṆU PAÑCAKAM)

Pāvanam sarvalōkēśam bhaktavañcitadāyinam
bhāvayāmi sadāviṣṇum sūryakōṭi samānanam

I meditate constantly on the Lord of all three worlds, Visnu, whose face is as effulgent as a million suns, who is most pure and who gives the devotees whatever they wish.

Samasta pāpanāśanam
bhujamgatalpa śāyinam
trilōkavandya nāyakam
namaskarōmi mādhavam

You who destroy all sins, who lie on the bed which is the serpent Adishesha, who are worshipped as the master in all of the three worlds, our humble salutations to the beloved of the Goddess Laksmi.

Mṛgēndravēṣa dhāriṇam
gajēndramōkṣa kāraṇam
surēndrasēvya vaibhavam
vibhāvayē ramēśvaram

I meditate on the Lord of Rama, You who incarnated in the form of the man-lion, Narasimha; who liberated the king of the elephants, You who are served by the king of the gods.

Kuśēśayākṣam ākṣayam
kumārgginām suśikṣakam
aghāsurādi bhañjanam
harim bhajāmi rañjanam

The undecaying one, endowed with lotus-like eyes, who disciplines the unrighteous, who destroyed demons like Agha, I worship that Hari who brings joy to all.

Anamgakānti śōṣaṇam
prapanna mōhahāriṇam
nirīhamīśam adbhutam
vibhāvayāmi mādhavam

You remove the delusions of those who take refuge in You, O ultimate wonder, Lord of all, free from all desires, I meditate on Madhava who excels the beauty of the God of Love.

Lasat karābja maṇḍitam
lalāṭakānti śōbhitam
suvarṇa kuṇḍalānvitam
vibhāvayāmi mādhavam

You are endowed with hands as soft as a lotus you glow with the beauty of Your forehead. I meditate on Madhava who wears golden earrings on His ears.

Kēśavāya mādhavāya śāśvatāya tē namaḥ
nāradādi pūjiṭāya śrīdharāya tē namaḥ

Salutations to You, O Keshava (slayer of the demon Kesha), O Madhava, eternal one, salutations to Sreedhara (who wears Laksmi on His chest) who is worshipped by Narada and other great devotees.

ŚAMKARĀ ŚIVA ŚAMKARĀ

Śamkarā śiva śamkarā
śiva śamkara rūpa maheśvarā

O auspicious one, Siva, embodiment of auspiciousness, O great God.

Śamkarā śamkarā śamkarā
śiva śamkarā śamkarā śamkarā

O auspicious one, Siva.

Ōmkāra priya śiva śamkarā
kailāsa priya śiva śamkarā
natajana priya śiva śamkarā
śiva śamkarā rūpa mahēśvarā

You who enjoy chanting the Om mantra, fond of Mount Kailas, the Lord of all beings, O Siva, the embodiment of auspiciousness.

ŚANKARJĪ KĀ ḌAMARU BŌLĒ

Śankarjī kā ḍamaru bōlē
śrī rām jay rām jay jay rām
mīrābāyī ki ēkatāri bōlē
rādhē śhyām jaya rādhē śhyām
jay jay rādhē śyām jay rādhē śyām

The dhamaru of Shankarji (Lord Shiva) sings aloud, "Victory to Lord Ram." The ektara of Mirabai calls out, "Victory to Radhe Shyam."

Śankarjī kā ḍamaru bōlē
śrī rām jay rām jay jay rām
tukārāmjī kī vīṇā bōlē
viṭṭhala viṭṭhala jaya hari nām
viṭṭhala viṭṭhala jaya hari nām
jay jay viṭṭhala viṭṭhala jaya hari nām

The dhamaru of Shankarji (Shiva) sings, "Victory to Ram." The veena of Tukaram declares, "Vithala, victory to the name of Hari."

Śankarjī kā ḍamaru bōlē
śrī rām jay rām jay jay rām
rāmadās kī kumaḍī bōlē
raghupati rāghava rājā rām
raghupati rāghava rājā rām (bōlō)
raghupati rāghava rājā rām

The dhamaru of Shankarji (Shiva) sings, "Victory to Ram." The kumadi of Ramadas calls out, "Sing to King Rama, to Raghupati, to Raghava."

Śankarjī kā ḍamaru bōlē
śrī rām jay rām jay jay rām
sūradās kī ēkatāri bōlē
gōviṇda gōviṇda jay gōpāl
gōviṇda gōviṇda jay gōpāl
jay jay gōviṇda gōviṇda jay gōpāl

The dhamaru of Shankarji (Shiva) sings, "Victory to Ram." The ektara of Surdas proclaims,"Victory to the Lord and protector of the cows, victory to the cowherd boy."

ŚARAṆAM ŚARAṆAM KĀLI

Śaraṇam śaraṇam kāli śaraṇam
śaraṇam satatam jagadambā śaraṇam
śaraṇam bhairavi bhadrē śaraṇam
śaraṇam satatam śiva śakti śaraṇam

Grant us refuge, O Kali. O Beautiful wife of Siva, please grant us refuge.

Pārvati śaraṇam pāvani śaraṇam
pāpa vināśiṇi mē śaraṇam
samasta viśva vidhāyaki śaraṇam
praśasta dakṣaki mē śaraṇam

Parvati, pure one, grant us refuge. Destroyer of sins, who decides the fate of the world, the daughter of Daksha.

Bhakta janāvana dakṣē śaraṇam
dukha vibhañjini mē śaraṇam
hṛdaya vihāriṇi karuṇā paurṇṇami
śaraṇam caraṇam mama jananī

Adored by devotees, You who destroy all sorrows, who dwell in our heart, the full moon of compassion, grant us refuge at Your feet, O Mother.

SARVAJAGATTINUM ĀDHĀRAM

Sarvajagattinum ādhāram
sanmayī nī sukhakēdāram
santatam enmanam aviṭutte
cintayil aviratam aliyaṭṭe

You are the substratum of all the worlds, You, who are the all-pervasive truth and the abode of all happiness, grant that my mind should always dissolve in the thought of You!

Nutanamennum nin rūpam
nitya vasantakatir pōle
mānasasarasin hamsini nī
māmaka jīvana cirabanḍhō

Your form is ever fresh, ever new, like the flower of eternal spring. You are the swan in the lake of the mind and the unfailing friend of my life.

Cintāmalarāl kōrttorumālyam
amba, ninakkāy cārttām ñān
tinmayakattān uṇmayilaliyān
cinmayī sanmati ivanarululū!

I'll adorn You, Mother, with a garland made of pure thoughts, O embodiment of knowledge. Bestow the proper intellect to guide me through all wrongs and dissolve me into the truth!

SARVA MANGALA

Sarva mangala lalitāmbika
bhakta manasa hamsika
bhaktimat kalpa rasika
lalitāmbika

The source of all auspiciousness, Mother Lalita, the illuminator of the minds of the devotees, You who are the Kalpa creeper to Your devotees, Mother Lalita.

Samrājya dāyiṇi
sadāśiva kutumbiṇi
bhavāṇi rudrāṇi
bhakta saubhagya dāyiṇi

The bestower of imperial dominion, the wife of Sadasiva (Siva, Rudra), who bestows happiness on the devotees.

Padmanābha sahōdari
bhairavi amṛteśvarī
hrīmkari īshvarī
rāja rājeśvarī

You are as a sister to Vishnu, immortal Goddess, in the form of the mantra "Hrim"; the ruler of all, You are the Lord of the king of kings.

ŚIVA ŚAKTYAIKYA RŪPIṆĪ

Śiva śaktyaikya rūpiṇī (3x)
amṛtapurēśvarī namō namaḥ

Salutations to the Goddess of Amritapuri, the union of Shiva and Shakti

Anitaramī bhava mōcanam
mama jananī tava cōdanam
anupadamī smaraṇam taraṇam
maraṇam vareyum śāśvatam

O my Mother, You liberate one from samsara and instill inspiration. Grant me the remembrance of You at every step until death.

Anavaratam kripatūkaṇē
anu nimiṣam śama mēkaṇē
tava caritam madhuram mahitam
sukhadam sumanō mōhanam

Shower me with Your grace constantly; teach me restraint every moment. Mother, Your story is sweet and sacred; it captivates the heart and bestows happiness.

Jaya jananī bhavatāriṇī
kaniyuka nī bhavahāriṇī
anupamamī sukṛtam hṛdayam
nirayum karuṇāsāgaram

Victory to You, who take us across the ocean of birth and death. Show mercy to me. Incomparable is the ocean of compassion that fills Your heart.

Ōm śakti ōm ōm śakti ōm (2x)

Mother, Mother, Mother

ŚIVA ŚIVA ŚIVA ŚIVA NĀMA

Śiva śiva śiva śiva nāma sumara nara
sakala manōratha pūraṇakāri
rāvaṇa nāma liyō dṛdha manasē
sakala dēvā āñjāsira dhāri

We chant the name of Siva, the fulfiller of desires. When Ravana took this name, all of the Gods became subservient to him.

Nandigaṇa japa sumirana kīnō
kāl pāś tat kālnivāri
upamanyū muni karē tapasya
dudh samudra kiyō badkāri

When Nandi and the Gunas prayed in this manner, they were released from the clutches of death. Sage Upamanyu practiced severe penance for Siva, who turned the ocean into pure milk.

Brahmānanda yahi vara māmgē
bhakti dāna dijō tripurāri

O Lord of the highest bliss, I ask only for this boon: grant boundless devotion to this servant of Yours, O Lord of the three worlds.

SŌKAMITENTINU

Śōkamitentinu sandhyē nīyum
ōrmmatan nīrattilalayukayō
sindūra varṇṇattil kulichu nilkkum nin
ullilum śōkāgni eriyunnuṇṭō

O dusk, why do you look so sad this evening? Are you also wandering at the shore of distant memories? As you burn with saffron color, is your mind also burning with the raging fire of grief?

Uṇṭō ninakkum orammayitupōl atō
kaṇṭō nīyumā snēha candrikayē
kaṇṭāl nīyum collumō śōkattāl
miṇṭān vayāttorente sandēśam

Do you also know the Divine Mother of the universe? Have you been bathed in that moonlight of Her infinite love? If you meet Her, please convey my message to Her, as I am speechless with sorrow.

Nalkumōyī puṣpadalaṅgal sandhyē
collumō ennuṭe vadanaṅgal
pōyvarumbōl collām ennuṭe
pōya vasantattin nalkkathakal

O dusk, take with you these flower petals when you depart. O, will you not convey my sorrowful words to my Mother? When I see you again, I will tell you many happy stories of bygone springs.

ŚŌKAMŌHA BHAYĀPAHĒ

Śōkamōha bhayāpahē śiva -
vāmabhāga nivāsitē
nāma rūpa vivarjitē śrita -
lōka pālana tatparē

O Devi, who stands on the left side of Shiva, who removes all sorrows and fears and is devoid of all names and forms, who is keen to protect those who seek protection!

Sōmabimba samānanē jita
pārijāta padāmbujē
hāranūpura maṇḍitē hara
pāpabhāram akhaṇḍitē

Your face is resplendent as the orb of the moon and Your lotus-like feet excel the parijata flower in beauty! You stand adorned with garlands and anklets; You cut asunder the weight of our burdens!

Candraśēkhara vallabhē jaya
bhanḍadaitya kulāntakē
bhaktamānasa hamsikē nija -
bhaktavṛnda niṣēvitē

O consort of Chandrashekar (Shiva who wears the crescent moon on His locks of hair), victory to You! The one who destroyed the race of the demon Bhanda, You are the swan in the lake of the minds of the devotees! You are the Goddess who is ever worshipped by Your devotees!

Āmayākhila nāśanē jaya
vārijāyata lōcanē
amba cinmayavigrahē kuru
mangalam bhuvi mamgalē!

Victory to You, who remove all afflictions, whose eyes are long, like the petals of a lotus flower. O Mother, embodiment of pure knowledge, auspicious one, bestow auspiciousness upon the world.

ŚṚĪ KṚṢṆĀ ŚṚĪ HARI KṚṢṆĀ

Śṛī kṛṣṇā śṛī hari kṛṣṇā
Gōvinda nandamukundā
gōpi lōlā gōpakumārā
vṛndāvana lōlā kṛṣṇā
nandalālā navanitacōrā bālā gōpālā
kṛṣṇā vēṇugōpālā

Krishna, Lord of the cows, son of Nanda, giver of Liberation, beloved friend of Radha, born of a cowherd family, fond of Vrindavan, stealer of butter, the young cowherd boy playing the flute.

Gvāline saba dūra gayī hē
kānhā hamkō bhūkha lagī hē
āvō kṛṣṇā cupkē cupkē
mākhana hē khānā
nandalālā navanita cōrā bālā gōpālā
kṛṣṇā vēṇugōpālā

The cowherds have gone far away. O Krishna, we are hungry. O Krishna, come, we have butter to eat. O, son of Nanda, stealer of butter, player of the flute.

Gōpiyā tujhē ḍūṇda rahī hē
raha tērī dēkha rahī hē
dhūm macānē rāsa racānē
ājāvō kānhā
nandalālā navanita cōrā bālā gōpālā
kṛṣṇā vēṇugōpālā

The Gopis are searching for You; they are awaiting You. Come, O Krishna, to celebrate the Rasa dance. O, son of Nanda, stealer of butter, player of the flute.

Tērē samgjō bītē hara kṣaṇa
kardē mērē mana kō pāvana
tērī līlāvōm kā varṇṇana
kaisē karūm kānhā
nandalālā navanita cōrā bālā gōpālā
kṛṣṇā vēṇugōpālā

Every moment spent in Your company makes my mind pure. How can I tell the stories of Your leelas? O, son of Nanda, stealer of butter, player of the flute.

ŚRĪ RĀMA JAYA RĀMA DĀŚARATHĒ

Śrī rāma jaya rāma dāśarathē śrī raghu rāma

Victory to Lord Rama, the son of Dasaratha, born in the Raghu clan.

Kalyāna rāma kōdanda rāma
sītā rāma śrī raghu rāma

The bestower of auspiciousness, who wields the bow, born in the Raghu clan.

Rām jay rām śrī rām jaya rām
śrī rāma jaya rāma sītā rāma

ŚUBHRA SARŌRUHA NILAYĒ DĒVI

Śubhra sarōruha nilayē dēvi
amṛtānandamayī jay mā jay mā
vīṇā pustakadhāri sarasvati amṛtānandamayī
mātā amṛtānandamayī jay mā jay mā

Mother of immortal bliss, O pure, bright light, emerging from a lotus, victory to Mother. In the form of Saraswati, Goddess of knowledge, You carry the book of knowledge and Your instrument the veena.

Sakala kalāmayī sarasijanayanē
amṛtānandamayī
śvētāmbaradhara sundara rūpē
amṛtānandamayī
ōm mātā amṛtānandamayī jay mā jay mā

You are the embodiment of all the fine arts, O lotus eyed one. Adorned in pure, white clothes, You embody a beautiful form. Victory to the Mother of immortal bliss.

Gāna vilōlē nāda śarīrē amṛtānandamayī
kāvyālāpa vinōdini jananī amṛtānandamayī
ōm mātā amṛtānandamayī jay mā jay mā

Your body is trembling and resounding with music. You are the Mother of poetic recitals. Victory to You, the Mother of immortal bliss.

Vidyā dāyini viśva vimōhini amṛtānandamayī
vijaya vara prada karuṇā vāhini
amṛtānandamayī
ōm mātā amṛtānandamayī jay mā jay mā

You bestow knowledge and attract the whole universe. From You flows the boon of victory, bestower of compassion, victory to the Mother of immortal bliss.

Vidhiśiva vinutē śāśvata sukhadē amṛtānandamayī
śyāmala varṇṇē śārada mātē amṛtānandamayī
ōm mātā amṛtānandamayī jay mā jay mā

You perform the acts of Shiva and bestow undivided bliss. O dark-complexioned Mother of knowledge, victory to You, the Mother of immortal bliss.

SVĪKARICHĪṬU MAMA MĀNASA PŪJA

Svīkarichīṭu mama mānasa pūja
saumye sadāśivē sarvvārtthasārē
sāmōdam sāyujyamēkunōrammē
sāmrājyalakṣmī namastē namastē

Kindly accept my mental worship, O ever-gentle Mother, You who always bestow auspiciousness, You who are the essence of all that we seek in life. Prostrations to You, Mother, the empress of prosperity, who gladly give us liberation.

Pakalōnte karavalli tazhukātta puṣpam
pavanan vanolikaṇṇāl kavarātta puṣpam
makarandavṛndam nukarātta puṣpam
manamāṇatennum praphullamām puṣpam

A fully blossomed mind is a flower that is not caressed by the sun's rays, a flower that is not stolen by the wind, a flower that the bees do not drink from.

Kāmattin karalēśam patiyātta cīttam
krōdhattin jvāla vamiykkātta cittam
rāgattāl taruṇiykkāyēkātta cittam
rājēśvarī nityam kuṭikollunnāru cittam

It is a mind that is not at all stained by desire, that does not send forth flames of anger, a mind that has not been given in love to a woman and in which the empress resides always.

Nirajīvitasāphalyamēkunna cittam
parabhāvukamēttam kotiykkunna cittam
niragunna pariśuddha snēhattin cittam
niramālikapōlambika cārttunna cittam

It is a mind that leads to fulfillment, a mind that yearns for the welfare of others, a mind that is full of pure love, a mind which the Divine Mother uses like a garland of blossoms.

Tikavuttaśakti ninnullil tannuṇṭe
nilatettiyalayāte mama mānasamē nī
dhīratayāy munnēruka lakṣyattilēykka
svārtthatapōy marayumbōl jagadambikayēttum

O my mind, the greatest power is right within you. Go forward boldly to the goal without wandering aimlessly. When selfishness disappears, the Mother of the universe will arise within us.

Sarvvārppaṇabōdham nilanilkkunnuṇṭeviṭe
garvvaṇgalakannīṭina śāntātmāvaviṭe
niruvacanātīta viśuddhamā jyōti
sarvēśvarī nṛttam ceyyunnuṇṭaṇgaviṭe

Where there is total surrender, there is a soul filled with peace, devoid of all pride. There is an incredible effulgence there, and in it the Divine Mother does Her dance.

Nī tanne ñānennabōdham valarnnāl
nityānandābdhiyil nīntikkaliykkām
nērāya jñānam paripūrṇṇamāyāl
nāviludiykkum śivō 'ham śivō 'ham

When the knowledge that, "I am none other than You," grows, one can swim in the ocean of ever-lasting bliss. When one attains full knowledge, the chant, "I am Shiva" arises on the tongue.

TAKUTIYILLĀ

Takutiyillā enakkum oru takuti vantatu
tāyuntan pillaiyenum uyarvu vantatu
mikutiyillai en sollil mikayumillayē
mēnmai nirai tāyunakku nānum pillayē

This undeserving one became worthy by becoming Your son. My words are not superfluous, nor are they faulty. My glorious Mother, even I became Your son.

Naṭantavayum naṭappavayum unarantaval nīyē
nālai enna naṭakkum ena arindaval nīyē
enna tavam nān ceytu inku vandēnō
un kayil pilaiyena initirundēnō

You are the one who knows all that has happened in the past and all that is happening in the present. You also know what will take place in the future. I don't know what penance I did to be cradled in Your sweet arms.

Karuvirkku uyir tanta kāliyum nī tān - en
kavitaikku porul tanta dēviyum nī tān
unarvukkul kalantirukkum uṇmaiyum nī tān
ūmai entan kuralāka olittaval nī tān

O Mother, You are Kali, giver of life to the fetus in the womb. You are the Divine Goddess who gives meaning to my poetry. You are the consciousness that enlivens my mind. You resound as the voice of this dumb son.

Annaiyuntan anpinil nān - aṭaikkalamānēn
ādiyantamatra unil aṭaikkalamānēn
śaraṇam untan pādam en aṭaikkalamānēn
sarvamum unakkena nān arppaṇamānēn

O Mother, I take refuge in Your divine love. I take refuge in You who are without beginning or end. Offering all that I have, I seek refuge at Thy holy feet.

Vallamai tārāyō lalitēśvarī
vāzhttiṭuvōm un padamē jagadīśvarī
lalitēśvarī amma jagadīśvarī
lalitēśvarī amma jagadīśvarī

O Mother Laliteswari, grant me the strength to be victorious O empress of the universe, I adore Your holy feet.

TAPTA MĀNASAM

Tapta mānasam ullilēntūm
dukha sāgaramente svantam
prēma sāgara rājñi nīyenn
ammayallennōtiṭallē
sarva lōka vidāyini
enn ammayallennōtiṭallē

Within this heart lies a vast ocean of sorrow. O Queen of vast and unconditional love, Lord of the whole world, please do not tell me that You are not my Mother. O please do not tell me that You are not my Mother.

Munnamētoru janma monnil
ventunīriya vēnalonnil
nin kaṭākṣamaṇiññiṭān ñān
ninnatāmoru pulkurunnāy

In a distant birth, I stood as a mere blade of grass, shriveled by the blazing sunlight. Thus did I thirst for Your compassionate glance.

Annu ninmizhi peyta pūmazha
ente karmmam arutta tāvām
puṇya pādamaṇaññitān ñān
pinne janmam eṭutta tāvām

The flow of grace, like a shower of flowers, bestowed by Your glance, may have cut asunder the bonds of my karma. Thus have I taken this birth to reach Your holy feet.

Svapna tulya prapañca nāṭaka
hrasvavēdi paṅiñña tonnil
colliyā ṭuvatinne nikkāy
vanna bhāgamitāyirikkām

Perhaps this is my destiny, this transient, dream-like, universal drama in which I am called to perform.

Satyamānasa saukya rūpiṇi
nityamen hṛdi tūkitunnorī
anpozhiññi vanillorāśrayē
śarmade [sumatē] śubhavigrahē

O Mother, whose form is truth and joy, there is no other refuge for me than Your compassion which You eternally shower in my heart. You are the source of all happiness, of noble heart and of graceful form.

TARUMŪLA NIVĀSINAM (ŚIVA PAÑCAKAM)

Tarumūla nivāsinam ādhiharam
taruṇārkka suśōbhana cārumukham
nikhilāgama śāstra vibōdhakaram
praṇamāmi śivam sakalārttiharam

Residing at the foot of a tree, destroying all anxieties, whose beautiful face shines like the morning sun, imparting the knowledge of all of the sacred scriptures, I prostrate to Lord Shiva, who shatters all sorrows.

Gaganāmbaravītam atītaguṇam
gajacarmadharam hatadaityakulam
bhuvanatraya pālanadakṣam ajam
kalayāmi śivam sakalārttiharam

Draped in nothing but the sky, beyond all qualities of plurality, adorned with the skin of an elephant, who destroys the race of demons and protects the three worlds, I meditate on Lord Shiva, the birthless one, who shatters all sorrows.

Pramathādigaṇairaniśam vinutam
praṇavārṇava madhyaga ratnavaram
mukhapamkaja nirjita candramasam
pranamāmi śivam praṇatārttiharam

To whom the Pramathas (a group of Shiva worshippers) and others humbly prostrate, the precious jewel in the midst of the ocean of the Pranava mantra, the splendour of whose radiant face shames the moon, I bow down to Lord Shiva who dispels the sorrows of those whose hearts open to Him.

Hathayōga parōttamam ātmavidam
tapanōḍupalōcanam agrabhavam
garuḍadhvaja sēvita pādayugam
kalayāmi śivam sakalārttiharam

Supreme even amongst those who are knowledgeable of hatha yoga, the knower of the Self, whose three eyes are the fire, the sun and the moon, who alone existed in the very beginning and whose feet are worshipped by Lord Vishnu. I meditate on Lord Shiva who shatters all sorrows.

Jaya śamkara śam kuru sarvagata
mama samkaṭanāśana pāhi śiva
yamasannutavaibhava bhīma bhaga
śamayākhiladukham anīśa bhava

Victory to Lord Shiva whose deeds are auspicious, all-pervading one, destroyer of my sorrows, please be gracious and protect me. Before Your glory even Yama, the God of death, bows down. O Lord Shiva, You alleviate all sorrows.

TĀY IRUKKA PILLAI

Tāy irukka pillai nōkalāma un
dayavirukka makkal vāṭalāmā ammā
nī irukka nānum varuntalāmā unnai
ninaittiṭum ullam kalankalāmā

Should the children suffer in spite of their Mother? Should Your children wither in spite of Your compassion? Should I be sad in spite of You, should the mind that thinks of You remain disturbed like this?

Uyirukka uyirāy nirkkum bhagavatiyē
ullakkōvil vāzhum ōmkāra rūpiniyē
payirukku nīrāgi pāyntē varuvāy ni
pārkkum iṭamellām niraintē iruppāy

You are the essence of life, O Bhagavati, You reside in the temple of the heart, O embodiment of omkara. Like water falls on the plants in the fields, please come to us. You pervade all places, whatever is seen.

Madankamuni kaṇiyē madhura bhāṣiṇiyē
mantriṇi ākavanta madhurai mīnākṣi
udaviṭavē varuvāy tiripura sundariyē
orunālum maravēn unnai purantariyē

O beloved of Madanga Muni, sweet-spoken one, all mantras are known by You. Madurai Meenakshi, come to help me. Beauty of the three worlds, I cannot forget You, O Purandari.

TIRAYUNNU ÑĀN NINNE

Tirayunnu ñān ninne avirāmamen
hṛttil uyarunna tirakalil marayunnu nī
tiranīṅgiyen citta jaladhiyil nin
vadanam vilaṅgaṇē vimalāmbikē amṛtāmbikē

I search for You, the eternal one. You have become hidden in the waves of my mind. May all waves subside and may the lake of my mind reflect Your enchanting face.

Anupadam kōrkkunnu padamālyajālaṅgal
amṛtēśvarī ninne aṇiyikkuvān
nirayum padāvalakkakamē padārtthamāy
maravunnu nī nityam abhayāmbikē amṛtāmbikē

To make this garland of poetry an offering to You, I thread it again and again, imperishable Goddess. You are the theme of all my songs, You who grant us fearlessness.

Smṛti maṇḍhalattilēkk uyaravē vismṛti
poḍimūḍi māyunnitātma bōdham
mṛti pūkiṭum mumba mama hṛttiluyarēṇam
amarārchitē mātā mahitātmikē amṛtāmbikē

The world of my memories is constantly attacked by forgetfulness. My self-awareness is covered by dirt and dust. Before this life is lost to death, appear in my mind, O Mother, You who are praised by Gods and men.

Amṛtābdhiyām ninnilaliyān kotikkunna
himabindu vāṇivan amalāmbikē
layakāriṇi ennilalavēkaṇē sadā
sakalārttha sādhikē lalitāmbikē amṛtāmbikē

Before You, the ocean of nectar, this one drop of snow wishes to be dissolved, O pure one. Into whom all things merge in essence, always pour Your compassion on me. You fulfill all desires, O Lalitambike.

TIRUMUKHA DARŚANAM

Tirumukha darśanam kaṇṭēn kāli
tiruvaṭi tāmarai paṇindēn
oru mukhamākavē unpukazh nānpāṭa
tirumukham kāṭṭiyē dēvi nī āṭa
kāli mahēśvarī amṛtēśvarī

Great Goddess Kali! I see Your divine face and bow down to Your lotus feet. I sing Your praise with devotion and You dance, showing Your beautiful form.

Pullukkum nīralikkum ponnarasi nīyanṭrō
puvitannil uyirellām pōttumtāy nīyanṭrō
nellukkul maṇiyāka irupatu un kanivanṭrō
neñcattil uyirāka nilaippatu un azhakanṭrō

Great Mother, everything is You. You are the life giving water even for grass. You are the Mother praised by all beings, the rice inside the paddy is due to Your mercy. It is Your beauty that remains as the life in the heart.

Calamkai oliyālē chañcalamkal tīrttiṭuvāy
sathiya vākkatināl achamē pōkkiṭuvāy
kalamkum idayattin kavalaikal pōkkiṭuvāy
karuṇai mazhaiyāka gamgaiyāy pozhindiṭuvāy

The mere sound of Your anklets is enough to remove the vacillations of this mind. Your soothing words remove all fears. Please bestow Your grace, which flows like the river Ganga, and remove the sorrows from this heart.

TŪNKA KARIMUKATTHU

Tūnka karimukatthu tūmaṇiyē
tūyavar manam nirai māmaṇiyē
māsukal nīnga manam enilum
maravātunnai tudippōmē

O Ganesha, O elephant-faced Lord, O supreme, immaculate one, You dwell as a precious gem in the hearts of the pure. Though I have no mental purity, still I do not forget to sing Your glories.

Unnai vaṇankāmal yārēnum
oru seyalēnum tuvankuvarō
anpāy sirupul alittālum
anaittum vazhankum ganapathiyē

Adorned with the face of an elephant, You grant everything to those who offer just a blade of grass with love. Will anyone start any new work without first worshipping You?

Paṭṭatupōtum ivvulakil nī
parivāy vantāl pizhaittiṭuvōm
perumānē un nōkkiruntāl
noṭiyil nargati vantiṭumē

I have suffered enough in this world, only if You come and shower Your grace will I be saved. When You look upon me with Your glance that is full of Your grace then liberation will come immediately.

Valliyai mirala chetadhu pol
yengalai mirala cheyyamal
inidhe kuraigal kalainthu yemakku
innarul purivay ganapathiye

Please do not frighten me in the same way that You frightened Valli, the holy consort of Lord Muruka. Lovingly remove all of our defects and shower Your grace upon us, O Lord Ganapathi.

TYĀGA DIYĀ TŪNĒ

Tyāga diyā tūnē vraja kō giridhāra
bani mathurā tujhē pyāri rē
kal tak jō thī pyāri rādhā
āja bani kyōm parāyī rē

O Giridhara, You have left Vrindavan. Now, Mathura has become dear to You. Until just yesterday, wasn't I Your "beloved." But today, how is it that I have become like a stranger to You?

Nisa dina tōḍī dahi kī maṭkī
tōḍa diyā āj dil kō rē
tērē liyē saba khēl hē giridhār
dukha na jānī mōrī rē

Every day You broke pots of butter. Breaking my heart didn't seem much different to You. For You all this is but play; You know not my sorrow.

Hē giridhārī hē avatārī
rādhā hṛdayavihārī

You who lifted up the mountain, You are the indweller of Radha's heart.

Nirmmōhī jō tum hō giridhāra
vraja kī yād na āyēgī
prāṇa nāth jō tum hō mērē
rādhā jī nahi pāyēgī

Dispassionate as You are, O Giridhara, thoughts of Vrindavan may not come into Your mind. O, You who are the Lord of my life, Radha shall not be able to live any longer without You by her side.

Jaba chūṭē mērē prāṇa hē giridhāra
apnī muralī bajānā rē
muralī dhunkī dhārā mē prabhu
miṭa jāyē tērī rādhā rē

At least when I am taking my last breath, O Giridhari, please come and play Your flute. In the stream of the music of Your flute let Your Radha merge in You.

UṆṆUM SŌRUM

Uṇṇum sōrum parukum nīrum
uyirkkum kkātum uraiyum nilamum
yār tantatu namakku yār tantatu
ādi antam ētum illā annai tantatu

The food that we eat, the water that we drink, the air that we breathe, the land that we live in, who has given us these? Who has given us these? The Mother having no beginning or end has given these.

Amṛtamāna ānandamayī
annai tantatu namakku annai tantatu

The eternally blissful Mother has given these.

Kāli mātē amṛtēśvarī
jagan mātē amṛtēśvaī

O Mother Kali, immortal Goddess, Mother of the world.

Āviyākkai jñāna kalaikal
nāvil pāṭum nādam ellām
yār tantatu namakku yār tantatu
kamalam ēvum tiruvāy vanta
annai tantatu namakku annai tantatu
amṛtamāna ānandamayī
annai tantatu namakku annai tantatu

Wisdom and art for the soul and mind, the notes of all music sung by the tongue, who has given us these? The Mother Goddess seated on a lotus, the eternally blissful Mother, She has given these.

Kadirum nilavum vānil varavē
kazhani śezhikka mazhayai inkē
yār tantatu namakku yār tantatu
kaiyyil vālum śulam koṇṭa
annai tantatu namakku annai tantatu
amṛtamāna ānandamayī
annai tantatu namakku annai tantatu

The sunrise and the shining moon which illuminate the sky, the riches of harvest which are nourished by the rain, who has given us these? The Mother holding the sword and the trident in Her hands, the eternally blissful one, She has given us all of these.

UN VĀSAL TĒṬI

Un vāsal tēṭi vantēn karpakamē
en vāsal nāṭi vantiṭuvāy ammā

I have come searching for the door to You, O Mother, do come searching for the door to me.

Munnālil ennenna pāvaṅgal ceytēnō
mukkaṇṇi ennai kākka ōṭōṭi varuvāyē

From whatever sins I have committed in the past, O three-eyed one, do come and protect me.

Anna vāhanattil ambikayē nī varuvāy
anu dinamum enakku arulmāri nī pozhivāy
unniru padamalar ōmkāri nī taruvāy
unaiye nambinēn umaiyaval kāttiṭuvāy

Mother, You come sitting on the swan to rain Your compassion on me each day. Give me refuge at Your lotus feet, O source of the syllable Om. I place my faith in You, O Goddess Uma, do protect me.

Petra thai ennai pēdalikka viṭuvāyā
pērarulai mayilai perumāṭṭi taruvāyē
karpaka malarē kāttiṭa varuvāyē
kapāli manam makizhum karuṇā sāgariyē

You are my real Mother, will You let me suffer like this? Give me Your greatest grace, O Devi of Mylapore. O flower of the wish-fulfilling tree, come here to protect us. O ocean of compassion, You make Shiva happy.

VĀGADHĪŚVARĪ

Vāgadhīśvarī śāradē varadāyinī
catur vēdarūpiṇi vāṅmayī amṛtēśvarī

O Goddess Sarada (Saraswati), Goddess of speech, dispenser of boons, You are the embodiment of the four Vedas and the essence of sound, O immortal Goddess.

Dēvā dēvā manōharī danujāntakī
śata kōṭibāla divākarō jvalarūpinī

The mind of the Lord of the Gods is enchanted by You, the destroyer of demons, whose radiant form shines like a million sunrises all rising together.

Nāma kīrttana lōlupē sura pūjitē
śuka nāradā dibhirarchitē natapālikē

Fond of devotional singing, adored by the celestial beings, worshipped by Sages like Narada and Shiva, You protect those who seek Your blessings.

Caṇḍā muṇḍa niṣūdinī raṇa caṇḍikē
jaya samkarāṅga nivāsinī lalitāmbikē

You destroyed the demons Chanda and Munda, on the battlefield You became the Goddess Chandika. Victory to You who reside on the lap of Lord Shiva, Mother Lalita.

Śumbha daitya vināśinī śivarañjini
bhava bhīti bhañjini dēhimē karunāmṛtam

Annihilator of the demon Sumba, enchanter of Lord Shiva, who dispels the fear in worldly existence, grant me the nectar of Your compassion.

Mangalam tava cintanam jagadambikē
mama vandanam padapamkajē amṛtēśvarī
[bhuvanāmbikē]

The remembrance of You brings auspiciousness, O Mother of the universe. I salute Your blessed feet, O immortal Goddess [O Mother of the entire Earth].

VĀṆI SARASVATI

Vāṇi sarasvati vaiśambāyani
vāgbhaṭa śundarī nāmōḥ namaḥ
dhavalām baradhara vēda svarūpiṇi
mangala kāriṇi namōḥ namaḥ

Saraswati, Goddess of speech, companion of Brahma, the beautiful Goddess of words, salutations. Clothed in pure white dress, O embodiment of the Vedic knowledge, Goddess of auspiciousness, I salute Thee!

Vīṇābhūṣaṇa tatpatarañcita
gānamahēśvarī namōḥ namaḥ
pāpavināśini prēmasvarūpiṇi
manalayaśāntini namōḥ namaḥ

You are the greatest Goddess, You enjoy playing the sweet music of Your Veena. Destroyer of sins, the ideal of love, You give peace by dissolving the restless and agitated mind, I salute You.

Samkaṭahāriṇi satgatidāyini
āśritarakṣaki namōḥ namaḥ
vidyā dāyini vimala svarūpiṇi
nirmmala gāyaki namōḥ namaḥ

You destroy all sorrows and grant us salvation. Guardian of those who seek Your protection, You dispense knowledge and You shine with purity. Your divine singing is without any blemish, salutations.

Sūndara śrūtilaya gītavihāriṇi
śrī vimalāmbikē namōḥ namaḥ
amalē vimalē ānanda rūpiṇi
dēvi sarasvati namōḥ namaḥ

Mother of purity, You who compose beautiful melodies, taintless Mother, radiating bliss, Goddess Saraswati, I salute You!

Jaya jaya dēvi vidyā dāyini
dūkha nivāriṇi vāgdēvi

Victory to Devi, who grants knowledge and destroys sorrows, victory to the Goddess of speech.

VARDĒ MĀTĀ JAGADAMBĒ MĀTĀ

Vardē mātā jagadambē mātā
bhakti kā dān dē mā
prēma kā dān dē mā
tērī kṛpā hō ham pē mātā
vardē mātā

Grant us a boon, O Mother of the universe. Give us the boon of devotion, give us the boon of love. O Mother, may Your grace be ever upon us, O grant us a boon.

Dāsa mē tērē caraṇō kā
mērē prāṇa bhī tūhī mātē

I am the servant of Your holy feet. You are my very life.

Mā tērē jaisā tō kōyī nahi
prēmamayī karunāmayī
śatakōṭi praṇām caraṇōm mē
vardē mātā

O Mother. There is none other equal to You, O embodiment of love, embodiment of compassion. A hundred thousand prostrations at Your feet.

Jisanēbhī mātā tujhakō pukārā
saba sankaṭa dūr usnē pāyā
jō tērē darbāra mē āyā
manamē śānti tūnē jagāyā

Whoever calls out to You, O Mother, he soon finds that all of his problems in life are leaving him. O Mother, whoever comes before Your divine presence, You awaken eternal peace in his mind.

Mā tērē jaisā tō kōyī nahi
prēmamayī karunāmayī
śatakōṭi praṇām caraṇōm mē
vardē mātā

O Mother, there is none other equal to You, embodiment of love, embodiment of compassion. A hundred thousand prostrations at Your feet.

VARDĒ VARDĒ JAYA VARDĒ

Vardē vardē jaya vardē
jaya jaya jaya śubha vardē

O, grant us a boon, hail the giver of boons.

Jaya jananī śubha mangala kāriṇi
saṅkaṭa hariṇī vardē
śaraṇam jananī tava pada śaraṇam
amṛtapurēśvarī vardē
śyāmala kōmala rūpiṇī mātē
rājēśvarī śrī vardē
pārvatī pāvanī pāpa vināśinī
rāmēśvarī śrī vardē

Victory to the Mother, the giver of auspiciousness, O, remover of all troubles, give us a boon. I seek refuge, O Mother, at Your holy feet, O Goddess of Amritapuri, bestow a boon. O, Mother of dark hue and pristine beauty, O Rajeswari, bestow a boon. O, Goddess Parvati, O pure one, You who destroy all sins, Goddess of delight, bestow a boon.

Janamana hāriṇī śrīkari rādhē
karuṇā lōlē vardē
naṭana manōhari natajana pālinī
śrī lalitē śiva vardē
mṛdu mṛdu hāsinī mañjula bhāṣiṇi
manasukha dāyinī vardē
manalaya kāriṇī mama hṛdi vāsinī
mama jananī jaya vardē

The stealer of the mind, performer of auspicious deeds, O Radha, compassionate one, bestow a boon. Enchanting dancer, protector of all beings, O Sri Lalita, give us an auspicious boon. One who smiles softly, one of sweet speech, O giver of peace to the mind, give us a boon. The cause for the dissolution of the mind, the indweller of my heart, O my Mother, give us a boon.

VARUVĀNAMĀNTRAM

Varuvānamāntram innenten ambikē
paitalin rōdanam kēlkkāññatō
piṭayunnu hṛdayam ninnuṭe vērpāṭil
takarunnu ñān talarunnu

Why are You so late to come, Mother? Can You not hear the cries of this poor child? My heart is struggling and breaking in separation from You, I am collapsing.

Ēkāntatayil ērunna cintayil
eriyunnu ñān piṭayunnu
viṅgumen hṛttil nin pratīkṣa tan kiraṇaṅgal
maṅgunu ñān kēzhunnu

Though in solitude, my thoughts increase; I am burning and struggling. In my grief-stricken heart, the rays of hope grow dim, anxieties grow.

Vaikarutammē ī kuññine kāttiṭān
ullil teliyukenn ammē
ente ī janmattin sāphalyam ennennum
nī tanne ammē nī tanne

Don't be late, Mother, to save this child of Yours. Please shine in my mind. You are forever the soul of my life.

VARUVĀY VARUVĀY GAṆAPATIYĒ

Varuvāy varuvāy gaṇapatiyē
valamai taruvāy guṇanidhiyē
iruvinai tannai nīkkiṭuvāy
iṭarkalai pōkki nalam taruvāy

Come, Come, O Ganapati! Grant us prosperity, O treasure chest of goodness, free us from the bondage of our past actions. Driving all obstacles away, bestow every good on us.

Śaktiyin makanām aiṅkaran nī
cañcalam tīrttiṭum śaṅkaran sēy
vittakan nīyē vimalanum nīyē
veṭṭriyai tandiṭa vandiṭuvāy

O son of Shakti, five-handed one, son of Siva, You are the destroyer of all restlessness, You are the creator, the purest, do come to grant us victory.

Akamum puramum iruppavanē
aṭiyavar tuyartanai tīrppavanē
mangala nāyakā mānava sēvitā
malarppadam maravā varam taruvāy

All-pervading one, You who remove all the sorrows of the devotees, O Lord of auspiciousness, served by all of mankind, please grant us the boon of not forgetting Your lotus feet.

VEṆṆAI UṆDA VĀYINĀL

Rādhē kṛṣṇā rādhē kṛṣṇā
rādhē kṛṣṇā rādhē śyām (2x)
rādhē kṛṣṇā rādhē śyām

Veṇṇai uṇda vāyināl
maṇṇai uṇda mannanē
unnaiyuṇṇa eṇṇināl
eṇṇai uṇda kaṇṇanē
gōpiyarkal tannuṭan

koñji vilayādināy
pāpiyarkal tannayum
gōpiyarkal ākkināy

O Kanna, with the mouth with which You ate butter You also ate sand. If I try to possess You, You are actually possessing me. You played with the Gopis and transformed even great sinners into Gopis.

Muttuppādal mālaikal
mukundanukku chūduvēn
muttumazhai pozhintoru
mona nilai kāṭṭuvāy
bhaktar pādum gītam kēṭṭu
paravaśattil muzhkuvāy
pārttu makizhum nānum unthan
parama padam kāṇuvēn

I will garland Mukundan with the garland of my songs. Shower Your grace upon me and bless me that I may know that higher state of silence. You become ecstatic by the songs of devotees. Happily seeing that ecstatic form I will attain to Your holy feet.

Kaṇkal pēśum vārttayil
karuṇai neñjam puriyudē
kaṇṇan kuzhal kēṭkayil
kaṇkal mazhai pozhiyudē
kala kala ennum sirippināl
garvamellām azhiyudē
karankal tarum aṇaippināl
kavalai ellām marayudē

The compassion of Your heart is revealed by the expressions of Your graceful eyes. My eyes shed tears upon hearing Your flute. My pride is destroyed by Your musical laughter and my sorrows are dispersed by Your hug.

Azhagu kaṇṇā en manam
un āyarppādi allavā
ādippādi kalikkalām
anpudanē nīyum vā
nandan unnil kalantida
prēma bhakti nalka vā
rādhākṛṣṇā sangamam
jīvan mukti allavā

O beautiful Kanna, isn't my mind Your Vrindavan? Come, let us play there together! Give me supreme devotion in order to merge in You. The union of Radha, the devotee, and Krishna, the Supreme, is that not the final liberation of the individual soul?

VĒṆU GŌPĀLĀ

Vēṇu gōpālā vēṇu gōpālā
nandakumārā navanīta cōrā
vēṇu gōpālā eṅkal bālagōpālā
yādavanē manamōhananē
mādhavanē paripūraṇanē

O Krishna, who plays the flute, O cowherd boy. The son of Nanda, the stealer of butter, darling cowherd boy. You belong to the Yadava clan, enchanter of the mind, O Madhava, You are established in fullness.

Nittiyammē nī nirguṇamē
nirmalamē nirai ānandamē
nittam ninpadam neñcil koṇṭu pāṭi tudittōm
kaṇṇā nintan nāmam cholli nāṅkal kalittōm
nīla mēgha varṇṇa nīyum ōṭi vā kaṇṇā
āyarkula mannā nīyum āṭivā kaṇṇā

Everlasting one, devoid of attributes, pure one, You are filled with bliss. Ever remembering Your songs in our mind we dance and sing Your praises. O Kanna, repeating Your divine names we play. O You with the complexion of blue clouds, come running. The hero of the cowherd race, come dancing.

Pullāṅkuzhal isai ūtiṭa vārāy
puṇṇiyanē vazhi kāṭṭiṭa vārāy
pīli tavazhum tirumuṭi tannai patri piṭippōm
muttuppavala īthal tanilē oru muttam padippōm
gōpiyarkal ēṅku kindrōm ōṭi vā kaṇṇā
kaikal kōrttu āṭiṭuvōm āṭi vā kaṇṇā

Come to play the sweet music of Your flute. Meritorious one, come to show us the way. We long to hold Your curly hair, which holds the peacock feather, and to kiss Your red cheeks. We Gopis are longing since such a long time. Come running, Kanna. We will dance holding Your hands, come to us.

VIDHITĀKHILA

Vidhitākhila śāstra sudhājaladhē
mahitōpaniṣat kaphitārttha nidhē
hṛdayē kalayē vimalam caraṇam
bhava śamkari dēśikā mē śaraṇam
amṛtēśvarī dēśikā mē śaraṇam

Best among all preceptors, knower of the oceans of nectar which are the scriptures, essence of the great Upanishadic truths, always do I envision Your pure feet in my heart. O Sankari, may You be my safe refuge. Immortal Goddess, be my sole refuge.

Viditā na mayā viṣadaika kalā
na ca kiñcana kāñjana masti gurō
data mēva vidēhi kṛpām sahajām
bhava śamkari dēśikā mē śaraṇam
amṛtēśvarī dēśikā mē śaraṇam

I don't know any art, nor do I possess even a single piece of gold. Nevertheless, bless me with that grace which is Your very nature. I surrender to You, O Sankari, may You be my safe refuge. Immortal Goddess, be my sole refuge.

Śarīram svarūpam yathā vā kalatram
yaśaḥ cāru cittam dhanam mēru tulyam
gurō ramghri padmē manaścēnna lagnam
tata kim manaścēnna lagnam tataḥ kim

The body appears beautiful and a wife is very attractive. Our fame may spread everywhere and abundant wealth may accumulate like the stable Mount Meru. But if the mind is not immersed in the lotus feet of the Guru, then of what use is all of this?

Ṣṭamgāti vēdō mukhē śāstram vidyā
kavitvādi gadyam suvatyam karōti
gurō ramghri patmē manaścēnna lagnam
tata kim manaścēnna lagnam tataḥ kim

All of the Vedas and all of the different sciences may be mastered and may remain ever present on one's lips, prose and poetry may flow forth, but if the mind is not immersed in the lotus feet of the Guru, then of what use is all this?

Jaya jaya dēvi jaganmayī nin pada
cinta hṛdanta vipañcitkayil
jaya jaya gītiyu tirttu kulirttu
jayikka sadāpati nirvṛtiyil

Victory unto You, O Goddess, universal Mother, let the constant remembrance of You play musical notes on the veena of my blissful heart.

Kanivōzhukum mizhi mañcu mṛdusmitam
amṛtoli vāṅmadhu māsmaranām
kara parilālana cumbana ātmana
kala vikalamba vimōhanamām

Your glance, overflowing with compassion, Your soft, enchanting smile and Your honey-like words are mesmerizing. Your caress, kisses and divine plays are enchanting.

VIṆṆAVAR PŌTRIṬUM

Viṇṇavar pōtriṭum vēdā
veṭṭri tantiṭum pāḍā
mannavar ṣaṇmukha nādā
mangalam enṭrumē nītā

O Lord of the Vedas, You who are adorned by the celestial beings, the worship of Your holy feet grants victory. O Shanmuka, six-faced Lord, please always grant auspiciousness for all of the earthly beings.

Giridhanai pilanta vēlā
kīrtti umai bālā
karimukan tambiyām śīlā
karumāri vēlpeṭṭrā śūlā

Son of the famed Goddess Uma, You split open the mountain with the spear gifted to You by Goddess Karumari. You are the younger brother of the dark-complexioned Ganapathi and You are the embodiment of good qualities.

Vēlavan tiruvaṭi tozhutāl
vinayelām ōṭiyē pōkum
mālavan marukan unnāl
manadinil inbam cērum

Prostration to Your holy feet drives away all evil fate and grants peace of mind and happiness, O Muruka.

Kumaranē guruvāy vandāy
kundramellām nī nintrāy
samaril arakkarai venṭrāy
saravaṇa bhava ōm tantāy

O beloved Lord! You assumed the role of the Guru. You established Your abode on the sacred hillsides. You victoriously killed the demons in battle and gave the mantra, "Om Saravana Bhava."

VIŚĀL HṚDAYA DĒNĀ DĒVI

Viśāl hṛdaya dēnā dēvi
prēm kē mārg pē cal sakē
svārth bhāv kō har kē ham
ōrō kē ghāv bhar sakē

Grant that our minds be expansive, O Goddess, so that we may tread on the path of love. Let us give up our selfishness and heal the wounds of others.

Śraddhā hamkō dēnā dēvi
vivēka kī dṛṣṭī rahē
apnē dharma kō samajha kē ham
apnē karma kō kar sakē

Give us loving alertness, O Goddess, so that we may ever have the keen vision of discrimination. Let us be able to understand our duty and accordingly perform our actions.

Viśvās pūrṇṇa karnā dēvi
nitya tṛpta avasthā rahē
hōyē jō vō ichā tērī
ēsā ham svīkār karē

Make our faith complete, O Goddess, so that we may always be content. Let us be able to accept all that happens as Your divine will.

Jay paramēśvarī jay jay mā
jay sarvēśvarī mērī mā
jay śivaśamkari jay jay mā
jay abhayakari mērī mā

Salutations to the supreme Goddess, salutations to the Goddess of everything, salutations to the Goddess, the consort of Shiva, Salutations to the Goddess who grants refuge.

VRAJ MĒ AISĀ

Vraj mē aisā mach gayā ṣōr
calē kanhayā jamunā kī ōr
rās racānē calē nand kiṣōr
dhūm macānē calē mākhan cōr

Vrindavan rose up in a tumult as Krishna walked towards the Yamuna River. The son of Nanda was going to dance the rasa lila, the divine butter thief was going to celebrate!

Muralī dhun bahnē lagī
dam dam dōl bhī bajanē lagā
śyām kō dēkh sab rah gayē dang
caḍ gayā unpē mōhan kā rang

The melody of the flute began to flow. The dhol (round drum) began to sound its 'dum-dum' beat. When they saw Shyam, everyone was spellbound. Their mood was coloured by the mood of the Lord.

Kānhā hē ēk gōpi anēk
kiskē sang vō racāyēngē rās
śyām kī yē līlā tō dēkh
vō hē khaḍē har gōpi kē pās

Krishna is only one yet the Gopis are many. How will He manage? With which one of the Gopis will He dance? O, look at this amazing play of Lord Krishna! There He stands by the side of each one of the Gopis!

Dam dam dam dam bājarē ḍōl
cham cham cham cham pāyal kī bōl
tāthaiyā tāthaiyā nācē sabhī
harī harī harī harī gāyē sabhī

'Dum-dum dum-dum' pulses the beat of the drum. 'Cham-cham cham-cham' ring the anklets. 'Thataiya-thataiya' dance the dancers. And everyone sings, 'Hari Hari Hari Hari.'

YAMUNĀ TĪRA VIHĀRĀ YADUKULA

Yamunā tīra vihārā yadukula tilaka nandakiśōrā
rādhāhṛdaya vihārā gōkulabālā gōpakumārā

O Krishna, playing on the shore of the Yamuna River, vermilion mark of the Yadhu clan, son of Nanda, You live in Radha's heart, O cowherd boy, protector of the cowherd.

Gōpī śata vṛta kṛṣṇā kāliya
damana kāmitavaradā
bhāmā rukmiṇi sahitā
śyāmala varṇṇa mōhana rūpa

You are surrounded by hundreds of Gopis, O vanquisher of the serpent Kaliya. You bestow desired boons, companion of Sathyabhama and Rukmini, O black-hued, glorious form!

Hari gōvinda jaya gōvinda jay jay gōpālā (2x)

Hari Govinda! Victory to Govinda! Victory to Gopala!

Karunā sāgara hṛdaya kavinuta
carita mangala sadana
nīlōl pala samanayanā nārada
vinuta vēdavihārā

O Krishna, Your heart is an ocean of compassion, Your story is praised by the great ones such as Sage Narada. Auspicious abode, Your eyes are like lotus petals. You are the one described in the Vedas.

Gītānāyaka dēvā dēvaki
tanayā tāraka nāmā
pītāmbaradhara śaurē pāvana
caraṇa pāhimukundā

O celestial being, the central character of the Gita, O son of Devaki, Your name gives protection. Grandson of King Surasena, You wear yellow garments, O pure feet, Mukunda, save me!

YĀVARKKUM TĀYĀNA AMMĀ NĪ

Yāvarkkum tāyāna ammā nī
yārenṭru śolvēnammā (2x)

O Mother, You who have become the Mother of all beings, how will I describe You?

Kamalamēvum tirumakalai enakku
kavitai tanta kalai magalai
imayavalli malai magalai enkal
idayam vāzhum alai magalai

O queen of wealth, You who dwell in the lotus, as queen of the arts, You bestow upon me the inspiration of rendering verse. O, daughter of the God of snow-covered mountains, You dwell in our hearts as the Goddess of purity.

Idaya kadavi tirantankē - nī
enakku kātchi tara vēṇdum
udaya vānil pēroliyai
un mukha darṣanam tara vēṇdum

O Mother, open the door of my heart and grant me Your vision. Your radiant face should become clear and brilliant like the full moon.

Ammā guruvāy varuvāy kāttarulvāy
amṛtapuri vāzhum enkal tāy

O Mother of Amritapuri, come to us as our guru and grant us Your protection.

Chalankai oliyai kēṭṭiṭavē - makkal
chañcalaṅgal parantu vidum
padankal paniyum vēlayilē - vīṭṭil
pāva vinaikal parandu vidum

As soon as we hear the sound of Your anklets all of our sorrows vanish. When we worship Your holy feet our sins will fly away.

Tāyēnna unnai charaṇ pukuntēn - ammā
dayavudan kāthu arul taruvāy
sēyēna enkal tuyar kalaivāi
cintai makizhntiṭa varam taruvāy

I take refuge in You as my Mother, kindly protect me and bestow Your grace. Accepting me as Your child, remove all of my sorrows and bestow the boon of happiness.

Chants

AMṚTĒŚVARĪ SUPRABHĀTAM

Unnidra lōka paripālana talparāyai,
san mañjumañcaśayanīya viniśramāyai,
vallīvanēśvarī, namō jagadambikāyai,
ambāmṛtēśvarī śubhē, tava suprabhātam

Good morning to You, Holy Mother Amriteshwari, the Goddess of Vallickavu, resting on a beautiful bed! Salutations to You, mother of the universe, intent on protecting the world that is asleep in ignorance.

Śuddhāntaramga samanirmmala cārugātryai,
śuklāmbara pratinavōjvala bhūṣitāngyai,
svōtsamga sīmni jagatām abhaya pradāyai,
ambāmṛtēśvarī namas, tava suprabhātam

Good morning to You, Holy Mother Amriteshwari, You are as pure and as beautiful in Your body as in Your heart and You are resplendent in Your spotless white attire and brightly sparkling jewels. In Your lap, You grant refuge to all the beings of this world.

Akṣairalankṛtakarām, rucitākṣahārām,
śvētāvaguṇṭanavatīm, vimalasmitāḍhyām,
vandē sadāśivamayīm, lalitāmbikām, tvām,
ambāmṛtēśvarī śubhē, tava suprabhātam

Good morning to You, Holy Mother Amriteshwari, whose wrists and neck are adorned with strings of the holy rudraksha beads. You are clad in pure white and You beam a guileless smile. Abode of the auspicious, You are the Goddess Lalitambika Herself.

Mañcādhirūḍha satatāgatavatsalāyai,
sañcārapūta bhuvanatraya viśrutāyai,
mātre namō "latāvana" maṇḍitāyai
āmbāmṛtēśvarī śubhē tava suprabhātam

Good morning to You, Holy Mother Amriteshwari. Seated on a chair, You receive with love Your children who constantly come before You. You are famous for Your travels that purify and protect the world. Salutations to You who are an adornment to Vallickavu, Your abode.

Dhanyābhidarśana kutūhala sanniviṣṭaiḥ
samstūyamāna kamanīya nijāpadānaiḥ
prābuddhyatē viṣayamātraratōpilōkō
mātāḥ stvadīya kṛpayā tava suprabhātam

Good morning to You who are surrounded by devotees anxious to receive Your darshan. Your charming exploits are here praised. Out of compassion, You enlighten even those who are totally immersed in worldly pleasures.

Nānā diśāgata sutairavalēpaśūnyaiḥ
avyāja bhakti vimalair vijitēndriyaiśca
sannyasya sarva mamatām tvayilīna cittaiḥ
āvēdyatē śivamayē tava suprabhātam

Good morning to You whose children, arriving from all quarters of the world, entreat You. Such children are devoid of ego and purified by their devotion. They have conquered their senses, renounced everything and immersed their minds in You.

Strīpumsabhēda gaṇanāvytirakta mārṣam
digbhēdaśūnyamatha dharmavibhēda varjyam
sarvam latāvana vihāriṇi tvaddidṛkṣā -
niṣṭham hi cētah ihatē śubha suprabhātam

Good morning to You. See how people of all religious faiths, hailing from all over the world, men and women alike, eagerly await Your darshan.

Samsāra dāvadahanārddita jarjaranam
antaḥ kṛpāmasṛṇa śītala dṛṣṭipātai
sāyujya sammita sudhām abhivarṣayantī
yā tēstu dēvī mahitē hita suprabhātam

Good morning to You. Your glances shower the heavenly nectar of compassion on those who have been completely overpowered by the burning fire of samsara, the cycle of birth and death.

Sūryēndu dīpra vimalārati pūjanaiśca
tvannāmakīrttana japā mukharai staramgaiḥ
sandhyāruṇārdra pulakō jaladhi stavārchā
niṣṇāta ityaha ha tē śubha suprabhātam

Good morning to You. The ecstatic ocean, reddened by the glow of dawn, is engaged in worshipping You with waves which resoundingly chant and sing Your holy name. The ocean offers You "arati" with the shining disks of the sun and the moon.

Ēkatra sāgara varōparatastu tīrttham
dvārāvatī sadṛśamāśrama matra maddhyē
viśvaika mātṛbhavanam hita kāṅkṣiṇām tad
addhyēṣi dēvī sujanaissaha suprabhātam

Good morning to You. Your ashram, with the ocean on one side and the river on the other, is equivalent to Dwaraka and has become the abode of the Mother for the whole world. Bestow Your blessings on it.

Vijñāmśca viśvaviditān vimalārdra cittān
amba tvadīya saralāmṛta vāgvilāsaiḥ

vismāpaya tyanudinam pradidēśayānaiḥ
ambāmṛtēśvarī śubhē tava suprabhātam

Good morning to You, Holy Mother Amriteshwari, who, traveling continuously all over the world, astonish the learned, the famous and the pure of heart alike with Your simple, nectarous and captivating words.

Ēkatra gānapariśīlana tūrya ghōṣaiḥ
anyatra mantrajapa yantra viśēṣamēlaiḥ
pañcākṣarī pranava mantra kṛtābhivādyaiḥ
sarvatra nāka subhagam tava suprabhātam

Good morning to You. From one side of Your ashram, which equals the celestial world in beauty, we hear singing and musical instruments being practiced. From the other side we hear the joyful chanting of mantras. Everywhere we hear greetings uttered through the mantra, "Namah Shivaya."

Jijñāsu rartthakṛpaṇaśca tathāthavārttō
jñānī tavāmṛtakaṭākṣa nimajjanēna
sadyaḥ prayāti sakalam svamanōnukūlam
ambāmṛtēśvarī śubhē tava suprabhātam

Good morning to You, Holy Mother Amriteshwari. The seeker, the miser, the sick and the wise all attain the fulfillment of their wishes when they bathe in the grace of Your sweet glance.

Kōnvastijātabhavanam bhuvanaikavēdyam
vismāpakam śamabhṛtām niyamānubaddham
tvāmantarā racitavāniha divyadhāma
ambāmṛtēśvarī śubhē tava suprabhātam

Good morning to You, Holy Mother Amriteshwari. Who but You has turned their birthplace into such an astonishing, divine abode? It is peaceful, traditional and yet it is still unique in the world.

Bhinnāspadau janakajāramaṇaśca kṛṣṇāḥ
tā vēka bhāva rasikau tvayi nātra tarkkaḥ
kālatrayam gatavatām bhavatām tvayādya
nītā kṛtam hi janatā tava suprabhātam

Good morning to You. There is no doubt that Lord Rama and Lord Krishna, who lived on Earth in different bygone Yugas (ages), now manifest equally in You. Although three Yugas have now gone by, You have led the people of the present age back to the golden age of Krita, the first epoch.

Śrī śankara prabhṛtibhiḥ paripāllyamānā
śuddhā suśikṣita munīndra paramparā sā
strīrūpayā gama viśāradayā tvayādya
sampōṣitā sunipuṇam tava suprabhātam

Good morning to You who are well versed in the scriptures. You skillfully nurture the pure lineage of Sages founded and protected by Shankara and other masters of the past.

Amba tvadīya caritam bahucitra mādau
kṛṣṇām vidhēyamakarōttata ēvadurggām
kim tē tathāpi mukharam mukhatāmra patmam
mantranvitam "śiva śivē" ti ha? suprabhātam

Good morning to You, whose story is wondrous. In the beginning, You made Krishna subject to Your will and then Devi as well. Why then does Your beautiful mouth keep uttering the mantra, "Shiva, Shiva" even now?

Sarvātiriktamadhura smanasaukumāryam
sarvādṛtaika jananī hṛdayāravindam
ya sayka mātra gata gōcaram amba tasmai
naivānyadasti ruciram, tava suprabhātam

Good morning to You. Anyone who has experienced, even for a moment, the transcendent beauty of Your sweet voice, which is the essence of the Vedas, and the love of Your motherly heart that is revered by all, finds nothing else in the entire world appealing.

Viśvādhimānamatulam pratanōti mātāḥ
śaśvattvadāgamavidhim samanupraviṣṭaḥ
śiṣya praśiṣya varasañcaya ityadamyō
mōdaḥ satām hṛdi mahēśvarī suprabhātam

Good morning to You. Virtuous men feel great joy seeing that Your disciples and their own lineage of disciples emulate the scriptural injunctions given by You and thus receive the respect of the whole world.

Arkkōdayōtsavajayadhvanināśramōyam
bhaktaiḥ sahasrakiraṇairiva tyaktajāḍyaḥ
tvaddarśanōtsukamudaṅmukha ēva tiṣṭha
tyambāmṛtēśvarī śubhē tava suprabhātam

Good morning to You, Holy Mother Amriteshwari. Sounds celebrating the arrival of the dawn are everywhere. Like the sun, the devotees are also up from their slumber. The entire ashram waits eagerly for Your darshan!

BHAGAVAD GITA 15TH CHAPTER

Śrī Bhagavān uvāca

The blessed Lord said:

Ūrdhva mūlam adhaḥ śākham
aśvattham prāhuravyayam/
chandāmsi yasya parṇāni
yastam vēda sa vēdavit//1//

He who knows the Peepul tree, which is said to be imperishable, whose roots are in the Primeval Being, whose stem is represented by Brahma, whose leaves are the Vedas, is a knower of the Vedas.

Adhaścōrdhvam prasṛtāstasya śākhā
guṇa pravriddhā viṣayapravālāḥ/
adhaśca mūlānyanu santatāni
karmānubandhīni manuṣyalōkē//2//

Fed by the three gunas and having the sense objects for leaves, the branches of the aforesaid tree extend both downwards and upwards. Its roots, which bind the soul according to its actions in the human body, are spread in all regions, higher as well as lower.

Na rūpamasyēha tathōpalabhyatē
nāntō na cādirna ca sampratiṣṭha/
aśvatthamēnam suvirūḍha mūlam
asaṅga śastrēṇa dṛḍhēna chittvā//3//

The nature of this tree of creation does not, upon mature thought, turn out to be what it seems to represent. It has neither beginning nor end nor even stability. Therefore, felling this firmly rooted Peepul tree with the ax of dispassion.

Tataḥ padam tat parimārgitavyam
yasmin gatā na nivartanti bhūyaḥ/
tamēva cādyam puruṣam prapadyē
yataḥ pravṛttiḥ prasṛtā purāṇī//4//

Diligently seek for that supreme state. One who attains to that state returns no more to this world. Having fully dedicated oneself to that Primeval Being, from whom the flow of this beginningless creation has progressed, one should dwell on and meditate on Him.

Nirmāna mōhā jitasaṅgadōṣā
adhyātmanityā vinivṛtta kāmā/
dvandvair vimuktāḥ sukhadukha sanjñair
gachantya mūḍhāḥ padam avyayam tat//5//

Those wise men who are free from pride and delusion, who have conquered the evil of attachment, who are in eternal union with God, whose cravings have ceased and who are immune to the pairs of opposites of pleasure and pain, reach that supreme immortal state.

Na tad bhāsayatē sūryō
na śaśāṅkō na pāvakaḥ/
yadgatvā na nivartantē
taddhāma paramam mama//6//

Neither the sun nor the moon nor even fire can illumine that supreme, self effulgent state. Attaining to that, one never returns to this world. That is My supreme abode.

Mamaivāmśō jīvalōkē
jīvabhūtaḥ sanātanaḥ/
manaḥ ṣaṣṭānīndriyāṇi
prakṛtisthāni karṣati//7//

The eternal life force in each body is a particle of My own being. It is that alone which draws round itself the mind and the five senses which rest in nature.

Śarīram yadavāpnōti
yachāpyutkrāmatīśvaraḥ/
gṛhītvaitāni sanyāti
vāyurgandhānivāśayāt//8//

As the wind lifts scents from their place of origin, so the life force in and controller of the body takes the mind and senses with it when it leaves one body and migrates to another.

Śrōtram cakṣuḥ sparṣanam ca
rasanam ghrāṇamēva ca/
adhiṣṭhāya manaścāyam
viṣayānupasēvatē//9//

It is while dwelling in the senses of hearing, touch, taste, sight and smell, as well as in the mind that the life force enjoys the objects of the senses.

Utkrāmantam sthitam vāpi
bhuñjānam vā gunānvitam/
vimūḍhā nānupaśyanti
paśyanti jñāna cakṣuṣaḥ//10//

The ignorant know not the soul that departs from and dwells in the body and enjoys the objects of the senses. Only those endowed with the eye of wisdom are able to see it.

Yatantō yōginaścainam
paśyantyātmanya vasthitam/
yatantō pyakṛtātmānō
nainam paśyantyacētasaḥ//11//

Striving Yogis are able to see the Self enshrined in their heart. The ignorant one, whose heart has not been purified, knows not the Self inspite of their best efforts.

Yadādityagatam tējō
jagadbhāsayatē khilam/
yacchandramasi yahcagnau
tattējō viddhi māmakam//12//

The light in the sun that illumines the whole world, the light in the moon and the light in the fire, know that light to be Mine alone.

Gāmāviśya ca bhūtāni
dhārayāmyahamōjasā/
puṣṇāmi cauṣadhīḥ sarvāḥ
sōmō bhūtvā rasatmakaḥ//13//

Permeating the soil, it is I who support all creatures by My vital power. Becoming the nectarous moon, I nourish all of the plants.

Aham vaiśvānarō bhūtvā
prāṇinām dēhamāśritaḥ/
prāṇāpānasamāyuktaḥ
pacāmyannam caturvidham//14//

Taking the form of fire lodged in the body of all creatures and united with their exhalations and inhalations, it is I who consume the four kinds of food.

Sarvasya cāham hṛdi sanniviṣṭō
mattaḥ smṛtirjñānam apōhanam ca/
vēdaiśca sarvairahamēva vēdyō
vēdāntakṛdvēda vidēva cāham//15//

It is I who remain seated in the heart of all creatures; I am the inner controller of all. I am the source of memory, knowledge and reason. I am the only object worth knowing through the Vedas. I am the father of the Vedas and the knower of the Vedas also.

Dvāvimau puruṣau lōkē
kṣaraścākṣara ēva cā/
kṣara sarvāṇi bhūtāni
kūṭasthōkṣara ucyatē//16//

There are two beings in this world, the Perishable and the Imperishable. The bodies of all beings are the Perishable; the embodied soul is the Imperishable.

Uttama puruṣastvanyaḥ
paramātmetyudāhṛtaḥ/
yō lōkatrayam āviśya
bibhartyavyaya īśvara//17//

The Supreme Person is yet other than these. He, having entered all the three worlds, upholds and maintains all. He is spoken of as the Imperishable Lord and the Supreme Spirit.

Yasmātkṣaram atītōham
akṣarād api cōttamaḥ/
atōsmi lōkē vēdē ca
prathitaḥ puruṣōttamaḥ//18//

I am beyond both the Perishable and the Imperishable, thus I am known as the Supreme Person both in this world and in the Vedas.

Yō māmēvamasam mūḍhō
jānāti puruṣōttamam/
sa sarvavid bhajati mām
sarvabhāvēna bhārata//19//

Arjuna, the wise person who thus realizes Me as the Supreme Person, he knows all and he constantly worships Me with his whole being.

Iti guhyatamam śāstram
idam uktam mayānagha/
ētad buddhvā buddhimānsyāt
kṛtakṛtyaśca bhārata//20//

This most esoteric teaching has thus been imparted by Me. Grasping it in essence a man becomes wise and his mission in life is accomplished.

Ōm tatsaditi śrīmad bhagavad
gīṭāsūpaniṣatsu brahmavidyāyām
yōgaśāstrē śrī kṛṣṇārjuna samvādē
puruṣōttama yōgō nāma pañcadaśōdhyāyaḥ

Thus, in the Upanishad sung by the Lord, the science of Brahman, the scripture of Yoga, the dialogue between Sri Krishna and Arjuna, ends the fifteenth chapter entitled, "The Yoga of the Supreme Person."

DURGA SŪKTAM

Jāta vēdasē sunavāma sōma
marātīyatō nidahāti vēdaḥ
sa naḥ parśadati durgāṇi viśvā nāvēva
sinḍum duritā tyagniḥ

May we offer oblations of soma to Jatavedas, the all-knowing One. May He destroy all that opposes us. May He, the divine Fire that leads all, protect us by taking us across all perils even as a captain takes a boat across the sea. May He save us from all darkness.

Tāmagnivarṇṇām tapasā jvalantīm
vairōcanīm karmma phalēṣu juṣṭām
durgām dēvīgam śaranamaham
prapadyē sutara sitarasē namaḥ

I take refuge in Her, the Goddess Durga, who is radiant in complexion and fierce in austerities. She is the power belonging to the Supreme which manifests itself as the plurality, the power that grants the fruits of one's actions. O Goddess, who saves us from difficulties, our salutations to You.

Agnē tvam pārayā navyō asmān
svatibhirati durgāṇi viśvā
pūśca pṛtvi bahula na urvī bhavā
tōkaya tanayāya śamyōḥ

O Fire, Thou art worthy of praise. Through noble means You rescue us from danger. May our homes become peaceful and abundant. May You bless all future generations.

Viśvāni nō durgahā jāta vēdaḥ
sinḍunna nāvā duritātiparṣi
agnē atrivan manasā gṛnānō smākam
bōdhya vitā tanūnām

O all-knowing one, You destroy all sins and carry us beyond all sorrow. You protect us just as one is taken across the ocean in a boat. O Fire, guard our lives, ever be mindful of our safety. May You wish for our welfare, as does the sage Atri, who constantly prays, "May all be whole and happy."

Pṛtanājitagam sahamānamugra magnigam
huvēma paramāt sadhasthāt
sa naḥ parṣadati durgāṇi viśvākṣāmadēvō
ati duritā tyagniḥ

We invoke from the highest plane of being the Fire God, the leader of all, He who is fierce and vanquishes all of our enemies. May He lift us beyond all that is perishable, beyond all duality. May He protect us.

**Pratnōṣikamīḍyō adhvarēṣu sanācha
hōtā navyasca satsi
svāñcāgnē tanuvam piprayasvās mabhyam
ca saubhagamāyajasva**

You who are lauded in sacrifices, may You bestow happiness upon us. You abide in the form and location of sacrifices, ancient and recent. O Fire, be pleased to grant us happiness, we who are Your own Self. Bestow good fortune on us from all sides.

**Gōbhirjuṣṭamayujō niṣiktam tavēndra
viṣṇō ranusam carēma
nākasya pṛśtam abhisam vasānō vaiṣṇavīm
lōka ihamādayantām**

O Lord, You transcend sin and sorrow. You pervade all sacrifices. May we, desirous of good fortune in material and spiritual realms, serve Thee eternally. May the Gods who dwell in the highest region of Heaven delight me, who engages in Your loving adoration, by granting me this wish.

**Ōm kāttyāyanāya vidmahē
kanya kumāri dhīmahī
tannō durgiḥ pracōdayāt
ōm śāntiḥ śāntiḥ śāntiḥ**

GURU STŌTRA

**Akhaṇḍamaṇḍalāka ram
vyāptam yēna carācaram
tatpadam darśitam yēna
tasmai śrī guravē namaḥ**

Salutations to the Guru who reveals the supreme, undivided essence that pervades this entire universe of moving and non-moving beings.

Ajñāna timirāndhasya
jñānāñjana śalākayā
cakṣurunmīlitam yēna
tasmai śrī guravē namaḥ

Salutations to the Guru who rescues us from the darkness of ignorance and restores to us the vision of knowledge and of the Truth.

Gururbrahmā gururviṣṇuḥ
gururdēvō mahēśvaraḥ
gururēva param brahma
tasmai śrī guravē namaḥ

Salutations to the Guru who is Brahma, Visnu and Shiva. The Guru is the Supreme Brahman itself.

Sthāvaram jamgamam vyāptam
yatkiñcit sacarācaram
tatpadam darśitam yēna
tasmai śrī guravē namaḥ

Salutations to the Guru who reveals the essence of all beings, whether they be in motion or still, alive or dead.

Cinmayam vyāpiyat sarvvam
trailōkyam sacarācaram
tatpadam darśitam yēna
tasmai śrī guravē namaḥ

Salutations to the Guru who reveals the pure intelligence that animates all of the moving and the non-moving beings in the three worlds.

Sarvva śruti śirōratna
virājita padāmbujaḥ
vēdāntāmbuja sūryō yaḥ
tasmai śrī guravē namaḥ

Salutations to the Guru whose blessed feet are adorned with the gems that are the revelations of the scriptures. The Guru is the sun that causes the flower of knowledge to bloom.

Caitanya śāśvata śānta
vyōmātitō nirañjanaḥ
bindunādakalātītaḥ
tasmai śrī guravē namaḥ

Salutations to the Guru who is intelligence itself, who is the Eternal, who dwells in everlasting peace and bliss beyond space and time, who is pure and who is beyond all sounds and vision.

Jñānaśakti samārūḍhaḥ
tattvamālā vibhūṣitaḥ
bhukti mukti pradātā ca
tasmai śrī guravē namaḥ

Salutations to the Guru who wields the power of knowledge, who is adorned with a garland of the gems of truth and who grants both material prosperity and spiritual liberation.

Anēkajanma samprāpta
karmabanḍa vidāhinē
ātma jñānā pradānēna
tasmai śrī guravē namaḥ

Salutations to the Guru who reveals the light of knowledge and thus destroys the evil fate that has accumulated during countless births.

Śōṣaṇam bhavasinḍōśca
jñāpanamsāra sampadaḥ
gurōḥ pādōdakam samyak
tasmai śrī guravē namaḥ

Salutations to the Guru, the water sanctified by the touch of whose feet dries up the ocean of illusion and reveals the true and only contentment.

Na gurōradhikam tattvam
na gurōradhikam tapaḥ
tattvajñānāt param nāsti
tasmai śrī guravē namaḥ

There is no truth as high as that of the Guru, there is no tapas higher than the Guru, there is no knowledge as high as His knowledge. Salutations to the Guru.

Mannāthaḥ śrī jagannāthaḥ
madguruḥ śrī jagadguruḥ
madātmā sarvvabhūtātmā
tasmai śrī guravē namaḥ

My Lord is the Lord of the universe, my Guru is the Guru of the three worlds, my Self is the Self within all beings. Salutations to the Guru.

Gururādiranādiśca
guruḥ paramadaivatam
gurōḥ parataram nāsti
tasmai śrī guravē namaḥ

Though He lives, He was never born; the Satguru is the supreme truth. Above all else in the universe is the Satguru. Salutations to the Guru.

PURUṢA SŪKTAM

Ōm sahasraśīrṣā puruṣaḥ
sahasrākṣaḥ sahasrapāt
sa bhūmim viśvatō vṛtvā
atyatiṣṭhad daśāṅgulam

He, the Cosmic Lord, the Purusha, with a thousand heads, a thousand eyes, a thousand legs, who pervades all this universe, He still extends ten inches beyond.

Puruṣa ēvēdagam sarvam
yadbhūtam yacabhavyam
utāmṛtatvasyēśānaḥ
yadannēnātirōhati

Whatever is born now and whatever is yet to be born in the future, all are He alone. Not only this, He is the controller even of the Gods, thus, He transcends the mortal state.

Ētāvānasya mahimā
atō jyāyāgamśca pūruṣaḥ
pādōsya viśvā bhūtāni
tripādasyāmṛtam divi

Such is His glory, yet He is much more than all of this. The entire universe of happenings and creatures constitutes but a quarter of Him. The remaining three quarters of His glory consists of the immutable consciousness.

Tripādūrdhva udait puruṣaḥ
pādō syēhā bhavāt punaḥ
tatō viṣvaṅ vyakrāmat
sāśanānaśane abhi

The three quarters of the Purusha extend beyond the realm of duality. The one quarter of Him comes again and again to manifest as the universe. Thereafter, He pervades all beings that eat and all that do not eat.

Tasmād virāḍajāyata
virājō adhi pūruṣaḥ
sa jātō atyaricyata
paścāt bhūmimathō puraḥ

From the Purusha was born the Viraad (the universe in unmanifested, but potential, seed form.) Identifying with the Viraad, the Viraad-purusha was born. That newborn One manifested as the plurality. Thus He created the Earth and the bodies.

Yat puruṣēṇa haviṣā
dēvā yajña matanvata
vasantō asyāsīdājyam
grīṣma idhma śarad dhaviḥ

When the Gods first invoked Purusha they considered Him as their very oblation, the spring season as ghee, the summer season as fuel, and the rainy season as grains required for such an offering.

Saptāsyāsan paridhayaḥ
tri sapta samidha kṛtāḥ
dēvā yadyajñam tanvānāḥ
abadhnan puruṣam paśum

For this worship, the Gods appointed seven supervisors and created twenty-one kinds of fuel. The very Lord whom the Gods desired to invoke in this worship, the Creator, was tied to the sacrificial post as the animal offering.

Tam yajñam barhiṣi praukṣan
puruṣam jātamagrataḥ
tēna dēvā ayajanta
sādhyā ṛṣayaśca yē

The firstborn, Viraad-purusha, was offered as an oblation to the sacred fire. By this divine act, the Gods, Celestials and the Rishis all became victorious.

Tasmāt yajñāt sarvahutaḥ
sambhṛtam pṛṣadājyam
paśugamstāgamścakrē vāyavyāna
āraṇyān grāmyāśca yē

From this all encompassing sacrifice, performed by the Gods, was obtained curd and ghee. Created from this sacrifice were insects born of air, animals roaming in the forests and the domestic cattle.

Tasmāt yajñāt sarvahutaḥ
ṛcaḥ sāmāni jajñirē
chandāgamsi jajñirē tasmāt
yajustasmādajāyata

From that all encompassing sacrifice, the sacred declarations, the mantras and songs of the Vedas were born. From that sacrifice was born the different poetical meters. From that sacrifice alone came the mantras of the Yajur Vedas.

Tasmādaśvā ajāyanta
yē kē cōbhayādataḥ
gāvō ha jajñirē tasmāt
tasmājjātā ajāvayaḥ

From that sacrifice came horses and all creatures with two rows of teeth such as cows, sheep and goats.

Yat puruṣam vyadadhuḥ
katidhā vyakalpayan
mukham kimasya kau bāhu
kāvūrū pādāvucyētē

When the Gods meditated upon the Viraad-purusha, in what ways did they conceive of Him? What emerged from His divine face? What came out of His two hands, His thighs and sacred feet? These are now described.

Brāhmaṇō sya mukhamāsīt
bāhūrājanyaḥ kṛtaḥ
ūrū tadasyayat vaiśyaḥ
padbhyām śūdrō ajāyata

From the face of the Viraad-purusha were born the philosophers; from His hands came the warriors; from His thighs came the merchants and from His feet came those of humble birth.

Candramāmanasōjātaḥ
cakṣō sūryō ajāyata
mukhādindraś cāgniśca
prāṇād vāyurajāyata

From the mind of the Viraad-purusha came the moon, from His eyes came the sun, from His mouth came Indra and fire, and from His breath came the very atmosphere.

Nābhyā āsīdanta rīkṣam
śīrṣṇōdyau samavarttata
padbhyām bhūmir diśaśrōtrād
tathā lōkāgam akalpayan

From the navel of the Viraad-purusha emerged the inner space, from His head the outer space and from His feet the Earth. From His ears, the quarters manifested. Thus did the world come into creation.

Vēdāhamētam puruṣam mahāntam
Āditya varṇam tamasastu pārē
Sarvāṇi rūpāṇi vicitya dhīraḥ
Nāmāni kṛtvābhivadan yadāstē

I have realized that Primal Being, resplendent like the sun, ever shining, beyond all darkness. He who, having created all forms and names, in His wisdom, exists as though functioning through them all.

Dhātā purastād yamudā jahāra
śakraḥ Pravidvān pradiśaścatasraḥ
Tamēvam vidvān amṛta ihabhavati
Nānyaḥ panthā ayanāya vidyatē

He whom the creator proclaimed as the Viraad-purusha, whom Indra, king of Gods, propagated in the four quarters of the universe, it is by realizing Him alone that the realized Masters became immortal in their own lifetime. There is no other way for liberation.

Yajñēna yajñamayajanta dēvāḥ
Tāni dharmāṇi pratimānyāsan
Tēhanākam mahimānaḥ sacantē
Yatrapūrvē sādhyāḥ santidēvāḥ

The Gods worshipped the Lord of all yajnas. Thus, the dedicated sacrifice of yajna became the noblest of duties. The heaven wherein all previous performers of such sacrifice dwell, that heaven awaits those who undertake such sacrifice now.

English songs

BLESS ME WITH YOUR DARSHAN MA (DE DARSHAN MA)

**Bless me with Your darshan, Ma,
fill me with Your grace, Amma.**

**What can I count on, whom can I trust in?
All in this world, Amma, passes away.
The only unchanging truth is Your love,
Amma, only Your love remains the same.
Jay Jay Ma (2x)**

**Take me in Your arms; hold me there always.
Awaken divine love; open my heart.
Let Your river of love flow through me
Amma, carry me beyond life and death.
Jay Jay Ma (2x)**

MOST BLISSFUL KNOWER OF TRUTH (ANANDAMAYI BRAHMAMAYI)

**O most blissful knower of truth, Mother Divine,
Thy luminous beauty will shine forever.
O most blissful knower of truth, Mother Divine.**

**All Thy children cry for Thee, Mother of tenderness.
Thy holy vision is but a glimpse of Thy power.**

**Beyond the splendor lies Truth in its majesty
with glory as endless as Thy love.**

**Religions around the world have certainly hurt mankind
by feeding the arrogance that lives in the mind.
All creatures upon the Earth share in Thy gift of life.
Thy essence is dwelling deep within each one.**

CLOSE TO YOU

**All I want is to be close to You.
Hold me in Your arms one more time.**

**If You will be the sky, I will be searching for wings.
Everything I do I do for You**

**If You will be the trees, I will rest in Your shade.
You are all the comfort that I need.**

**If You will be my tears, I will be grateful for sorrow.
Deep inside the pain I feel Your love.**

**If You will be the wind, I'll be an open sail.
Helpless I am waiting here for You.**

**If You will be the rain, I'll be in love with the clouds.
You're the answer to my deepest prayer**

If You'll be in my dreams, I will cherish the coming of darkness. Seeing You I slowly lose all fear.
If You will be the song, I will fill my life with music.

Everything I feel comes from You.

COME CHILDREN (OMKARA DIVYA PORULE)

Come children leave all your sorrow,
find the Truth that is dwelling within you.
OM is the essence of all you are searching for.
OM is your own true nature. OM.....

Peace can be found in the stillness
of a mind that knows only silence.
Aim every thought at the goal of eternal Truth,
let not your path ever waiver.

Children beware of your actions,
every seed that you plant you must harvest.
Strive to become always loving and kind,
and the fruit that you taste will be tender.

All of this world is maya,
weaving powerful spells of illusion.
What is not real appears as the truth
in the clever disguise of ego.

**Be not enchanted with praises,
nor let there be words that offend you.
All that you need to remain ever calm
is a heart full of love and devotion.**

**Search for your life's true meaning.
Never feel it's an endless journey.
Just as a candle blown out by the wind
any moment your life may be over.**

**Children, Divine is your nature.
Never grieve for the past or the future.
Fear not for Mother is holding your hand.
Break this illusion of sorrow.**

COMFORT ME (ANANTA MAMI)

**O Holy Mother comfort me.
Let me hear You once more whisper my name.
Lonely and helpless like dust in the wind,
I'm lost in this infinite world.**

**My burdens are many my pleasures are few.
Why is it fate always takes me from You?
Long have I waited to see You again.
Promise me You'll never go.**

**Lead me to truth on a path that is sure.
Bless me with thoughts that are gentle and pure.
Free my mind from blinding pride,
I will be humbly Yours.**

**Only from You can my heart learn to sing.
Grace is the sun that reveals everything.
Grant me solitude to contemplate Thee,
shining before me again.**

DIVINE MOTHER AND FATHER (TWAMEVA MATA)

**Divine Mother and Father You are to the soul.
Both family and friend in Your arms can be known.
You have all wisdom and wealth in Your love.
It is all that a heart ever dreamed to behold.**

EVERY BIRD IN A CAGE

**Every bird in a cage always dreams of its freedom
and sings its song imagining the sky.
When Your love opens wide all the doors to my heart
then my soul will learn to fly.
Jay Ma (6x)**

**I am lost in the wilderness of sorrow and confusion,
stumbling I cry out Your name.
As the moon lights the path for the lone and weary traveler
I need Your Grace to show me the way.
Jay Ma (6x)**

**In the arms of my Mother I'm a child fast asleep,
safely cradled in Her warm embrace.
From the tempest of my mind I am desperate for relief,
Amma, once more let me look into Your face.
Jay Ma (6x)**

GIVE ME REFUGE (ABHAYAM TAN ARULUKA)

**Give me refuge and appear within me.
Grant me this prayer my beloved Krishna.
Like the full moon bright in the night sky,
shine in my heart forever.**

**Your grace is a shower of ambrosia
to quench the embers of my sorrow.
You are the Essence of Truth,
please bless me with Thy vision.**

**I'm a stranger lost in the forest
with no one to share this lonely journey.
Comfort me with Thy grace Sri Krishna.
You are the Ocean of Compassion.**

**That the lamp of love may burn brightly,
pull up the wick dearest Krishna.
Like the sweetest flowers in nature,
let me see Thy feet before me.**

GIVE US GRACE (SHAKTI DE BHAKTI DE)

Give us grace, give us love, Mother hear our prayer.
Grant us strength for devotion, innocent and pure.

Free us to merge with You. Just a gaze will lift our soul.
Please fill our wish today, have compassion Amma.

Held in the grand illusion, we are restless for Truth.
Will You light the lamp of knowledge, and give inner peace?

Caught in the sea of dreams, deeper than a mind can hold.
Your light brings higher purpose, blessing simple hearts.

Bless us with Your grace. Bring us to Your peace.
Teach us with Your song. Hold us in Your love.

I'M LONGING FOR YOU (MILNA TUJHE)

O Amma, I'm longing for You.
Please tell me what to do with this heart.
I am longing to be near You.
Your Children cannot forget You.

Once You've held them and dried their tears, Amma?
Once You've held them, they can't forget You.

Have You always been with me,
guiding me throughout eternity?
Have You always been with me, buried deep inside?
Can Your children ever forget You, Amma?

Once they have tasted Your love? Amma, they can't forget You.
Amma is a sea of mercy,

forgiving everyone completely.
Amma, Your heart is endless,
giving love so selflessly.
Your children wait for love.
They are crying all alone in their pain
But Amma will not forget them.

IN THE STILL OF THE NIGHT (RAJA RAM)

In the still of the night, from the darkness comes a light.
And I know in my heart it is You. (2x)

When the fire in my soul burns with longing for the goal,
Then I know in my heart it is You. (2x)

When the Truth is revealed all the sorrow will be healed,
And I'll know in my heart it is You. (2x) Jay ma.

KRISHNA PLAY WITH US (VINATI HAMARI)

Have you heard us calling for You?
Krishna, are You hiding?
Can You tell us if we have done wrong?
Please come back and tease us.

Living fire of ecstasy is in Your devotion.
Take us to the place where You live, eternal sweetness.
Krishna come, Krishna come,
Krishna come play with us.

We have waited through the night.
Are You coming Krishna?
We are captured by Your beauty,
we're crying for You.

Please won't You return to dance,
even for a moment?
Life becomes so dreary, Krishna,
without divine mystery.

LET MY SPIRIT FLY TO YOU

**Let my spirit fly to You.
No place could be too far.
Remove this cloud of ignorance
and show me where You are.**

**Let my spirit sing to You
of voices no one hears.
Of those who suffer silently,
no one to wipe their tears.**

**Let my spirit dance with You.
In Your arms I have no fear.
The rhythm of Your graceful step
is all I want to hear.**

**Let my spirit pray to You.
Let hunger soon be gone.
Let hate and anger disappear
as darkness at the dawn.**

**Let my spirit bow to You
as the Earth beneath Your feet.
The essence of humility
is found in love so sweet.**

**Let my spirit merge with
You as a wave into the sea.
I hear You softly whispering,
come home my child be free.**

LIGHT OF TRUTH (BANDHAM ILLA)

No one sees that all we have
will one day disappear.
At the time of death your sole companion
is the light of truth.

Sadly, we keep holding on
to what was never ours,
We forget that on the final journey
all have empty hands.

If you yearn to know what is real,
turn your gaze within,
for the essence of the universe
is living in your soul.

There the self shines like a jewel,
glorious and pure.
Come and find the place that has no sorrow,
only love is there.

Selfishness and ignorance
have spoiled the heart of man.
Only when the storm of ego passes,
knowledge then will dawn.

Find the purpose of your life
as a river finds the sea.
To love and to serve all living beings
is to become free.

LIVING GODDESS (VISHVA MANAVA)

**Living Goddess with enchanting beauty,
You have charmed all humanity.
All Your life is a sacred message,
full of love and humility.**

**In my heart are a thousand prayers.
In my mind are a thousand songs.
In my soul there's only silence,
dreaming of Thy holy Form.**

**O how brilliant is Thy presence.
All the heavens bow to Thee.
In the song of life eternal,
You're the precious melody.**

**In the sunshine of Your smile,
pure compassion floods the world.
Goodness blooms like tender flowers
in the hearts of everyone.**

MOTHER OF IMMORTAL BLISS (SNEHAMRITANANDANI)

**Mother of immortal bliss,
gently reverent in robes soft and white,
Master of wisdom and charm,
Amma, supreme Goddess divine.**

**Amma, enchanting Mother of bliss,
You hold us in universal love.
Rivers of nectar flow from Your heart.
You show us the true Essence of Om.**

**You have compassion for all,
giving meaning to supreme love.
Your music celebrates with prayer.
You are divinely radiant with grace.**

**Knower of ancient truth,
deep awareness filled with joy.
Ambrosia for every soul,
ever peaceful, the goal of our heart.**

**Aware of each one's need,
a creative dance of light.
Oneness that liberates the mind,
Amma, living blossom of truth.**

MOTHER SEND YOUR LOVE TO ME

**The sun is drowning in the western sea,
another day gone by.**

**Mother send Your love to me
and wipe these tears from my eyes.**

**Day after day I go on like this,
an empty-hearted fool.**

**When will You give me a taste of the bliss
so deep inside of You?**

Mother please give me a taste of the bliss
so deep inside, so deep inside of You.

Must I grow older in this loneliness
so far apart from You?

To end this longing and this emptiness -
Mother what more can I do?

Why did I take this human birth
if You won't set me free?

The sun, My eyes, this whole Earth,
we're drowning in Your sea.

Mother what more can I say to You
so You will understand?

My heart, my hopes, my whole life too,
they're resting in Your hand.

RISE UP MOTHER KALI (JAGO MA)

Rise up, Mother Kali, arise.
Rise up, Mother Kali, arise.

My thoughts and desires are overpowering me.
They will carry me away; they will imprison me.
Yet one glance from You, Kali, will drive them away.
Kali, rise up and save me. Come and rescue Your child.

Won't You show Your compassion and come to my aid?
Are You sleeping, dear Kali, or testing my faith?
If You don't save me, all will say my mother has no heart.
Kali, rise up and save me. Come and rescue Your child.

TAKE ME DEEP IN YOUR EYES

Take me deep in Your eyes, far away from my life,
to the place where we all become nothingness.
Take me deep in Your eyes, far away from my mind,
to the place where we all merge with everything.

Everywhere You go, I will be there with you.
No matter if it looks like I am here.
I have placed my heart, like a flower, at Your feet.
This night of sorrow ends when You are near

All throughout my life, I have cherished just one dream,
the dream of knowing love that is divine.
When Your magic smile reached deep into my soul,
the tender light of hope began to shine.

Many tears have fallen on the ground where You have stood;
I'm drifting in a sea of memories.
Faith is my sole friend as I wait for Your return
and listen for Your voice in every breeze.

**Some pray for salvation, some pray to be healed,
some will pray to realize the Truth.
Every night and day like a song that has no end,
I pray that I may always be with You.**

THE SWEETNESS OF DEVOTION

**The sweetness of devotion,
like a gentle morning rain,
Will cleanse the heart of selfishness
and wash away the pain.**

**The fear of separation,
like shadows in the night,
will vanish as the dawn of Truth
reveals its golden light.**

**The tears that come from longing
flow like rivers made of fire.
They burn into my aching heart
like embers of desire.**

**The secret of surrender
lives in children everywhere.
They love the world with innocence,
and laughter that they share.**

**To all who wish for happiness,
remember what is true,
the love you give with every breath
will soon return to you.**

YOU'RE THE ESSENCE (ULLAKATTIN ADHARA)

Mother, You're the essence
that lives in everything.
You're the source of inspiration
only love can bring.

In this world of pain and sorrow,
You bring only joy.
Guiding all with perfect wisdom
You are Truth Divine.

Take me by the hand, Amma;
show me how to be.
Come and dwell inside my heart
for all eternity.

I have seen the tender mercy
deep inside Your eyes.
Bathe me in Your sweet compassion,
treasure of my life.

Index of Bhajans Volume 4

www.ingramcontent.com/pod-product-compliance
Lightning Source LLC
Chambersburg PA
CBHW071212090426
42736CB00014B/2788
* 9 7 8 1 6 8 0 3 7 0 2 4 9 *